D0929867

Law in Society Series

NEGOTIATED JUSTICE

Negotiated Justice

PRESSURES TO PLEAD GUILTY

John Baldwin & Michael McConville

Law in Society Series
edited by C. M. CAMPBELL and P. N. P. WILES

Martin Robertson

First published in 1977 by Martin Robertson & Company Ltd, 17 Quick Street, London N1 8HL

ISBN 0 85520 171 1

Filmset in Great Britain by
Northumberland Press Ltd, Gateshead, Tyne and Wear,
and printed by Richard Clay (The Chaucer Press) Ltd,
Bungay, Suffolk

CONTENTS

INTRODUCTORY NOTE

In 1974 it was announced that a large-scale study concerned with the outcome of jury cases in the Crown Court was to be carried out. The Home Office agreed to fund the study, and a Consultative Committee to advise on the research project was established. The research was to be done by members of staff at the Institute of Judicial Administration in Birmingham. This monograph details the findings to emerge from one part of the research study. As such it may claim to be both an important and a controversial publication.

A large part of the research reported here was concerned with examining the extent to which 'plea bargaining' occurred in the Birmingham Crown Court. Although the tactic of plea bargaining is known to be widely used (and well reported and researched) in the United States, it has been popularly held to be used only very sparingly in England, and even then only under rigid and carefully circumscribed conditions. There was however no firm or reliable knowledge as to the exact extent of plea bargaining in England, or the precise forms which it can take. This research provides the first detailed empirical examination of the issues and problems involved. Some of the questions which the research addresses, and the methods used to try and answer them, may seem unremarkable to those acquainted with the literature in socio-legal studies. Indeed some of the answers which the research provides may be less than astonishing to those familiar with the work of the Crown Courts.

Nevertheless this is a very unusual book. Leaks in the press about the research have led normally sober 'leaders' of the legal profession into making comments which can only be described as vituperative. In a letter to the *Daily Telegraph* the President of the Law Society, Mr Napley, referred to 'what is euphemistically called "research"', and in resigning from the Consultative Committee he stated that it is 'wholly improper to present a document of this nature as if it were a piece of reliable research'. Mr Webster, Chairman of the Bar, stated in a letter to *The Times* that the report 'cannot possibly be described as "research"'. Both these gentlemen have campaigned, privately and publicly, to try to stop the publication of the report. Press comment became widespread when Mr Napley resigned from the Consultative Committee in public protest. On 15 March 1977, Mr Webster wrote to the Home Secretary stating, *inter alia*, that 'in my view it would be directly contrary to the public interest that the book should be published in its proposed form at this stage'. It is also an unusual book because on 18 May 1977, the Home Secretary, Mr Merlyn Rees, gave a lengthy written reply in the House of Commons to a question about publication of the research and the representation against publication which he had received from the legal profession.

Since they form part of the public representations of the two branches of the legal profession, comments on research such as those above have to be treated seriously. For the two researchers involved, Dr John Baldwin and Dr Michael McConville, the only defence against attacks on their research is public and academic evaluation of their work. As long as their work remained unpublished they were denied the ability adequately to defend themselves. The present monograph, with the exception of some very minor textual changes made at the suggestion of academic colleagues, is the complete report. The reader can now judge for himself the quality of the research work and whether the arguments against publication were justified.

Some of the detailed squabbles which surrounded this report need not detain us here since they are of little general interest. However some arguments raised issues about research in general, and about research into law in particular; these deserve some discussion since they concern or impinge on the whole area of research to which the *Law in Society* series is dedicated. Let us begin by summarising what the current research claims to show.

Briefly the research suggests that plea bargaining is not unusual in the Birmingham Crown Court, that the bargains which are negotiated by counsel may not always be manifestly in the defendant's interests, and that the processes which lead to the bargain being struck may sometimes go beyond what English law has so far publicly acknowledged. It further suggests that from the defendant's point of view the process of bargaining may be perceived as involving pressure to plead guilty to charges of which they regard themselves as innocent; as a result they may believe that they have been unjustly treated. The authors argue that these factors are a consequence of the institutional structure of criminal law and of the operations of the criminal courts.

Let us deal first with the argument that these results are particular to the courts and cases studied, and are not generalisable. Part of the answer to this objection is that all scientific attempts to produce knowledge have, as a matter of practicality, to rely on inference from samples to the generality. If we did not recognise this then we would be unable ever to generalise about any population of events, unless we had examined each (and every) individual event making up that population. Such a restriction, if applied to ongoing events such as court cases, would in principle rule out any generalisations. If we allow generalisations from samples, then the issue becomes whether there are acceptable arguments for generalising from a particular sample or a particular case study. If the pressures on defendants to plead guilty, which the present research details, were *merely* a consequence of idiosyncratic behaviour on the part of barristers working in Birmingham then they would be of little significance and there would be little grounds for generalising the results. However it is argued in this monograph that such pressures are a product of the structure of the legal process in criminal cases, and in so far as this structure is general to English legal process then the findings of the research are also likely to be general.

This of course still leaves us with an inference. For this research—as with similar research—there is room for and much to be gained from attempts at replication in other courts. At the least this research focuses our attention on issues which merit further research. It may also indicate an area in the criminal process that needs reform.

One of the arguments put forward by the Bar against publication of the present report was that if the researchers discovered that some defendants had been pressured into pleading guilty, then their duty was to advise such defendants of their right to appeal against their conviction, and to inform them of their right to complain against their barrister. There are both practical and moral problems if researchers were to follow this advice. The aim of research is to try and describe as objectively as possible a particular social process, and to try and explain why it operates in the way it does. Attempts to change parts of that process believed to be wrong, whilst conducting the research, would alter the process itself and so deny the goal of research. For researchers to hold out a hope that individual wrongs would be corrected may lead to exaggerated claims of injustices, and would divert the researcher from his task of trying to discover whether dissatisfaction with the process being studied is general, and attempting to explain why it occurs. In addition most social research, including the present study, depends upon promising all those involved that their identity will not be revealed, and that everything that they tell the researcher will be treated in the strictest confidence. For the researchers to have pursued individual cases of apparent injustice would have necessarily involved breaking both these promises. It is because of such promises that reports of research are always written in such a way that the individuals and cases involved cannot be identified.

On the wider moral question, research, in so far as it is concerned with social change as well as seeking truth, aims at producing knowledge which can be used as the basis for general reform. There is a conflict between correcting individual injustice which has become known, and trying to

x

discover whether a social process may be producing a series of injustices which would otherwise remain hidden. Researchers have no monopoly on moral action, but they certainly try and behave as moral actors whilst conducting their research. The focus of the moral action may be different from that of other groups, but their activity may do as much to forward the cause of justice as those who focus on individualised wrongs. It does seem important that this is borne in mind when research, and sometimes the researchers, are criticised when it becomes clear what the *findings* of a hitherto uncontroversial project might seem to suggest, imply, or prove.

Finally let us turn to an issue which will always be a problem for those researching into criminal law, namely can you believe statements made by convicted criminals? Any research which takes account of defendants' beliefs would clearly be impossible if all statements by those convicted were *a priori* denied any authenticity. In practice what researchers attempt to do is to build as many cross-checks and independent tests of defendants' statements into their research as is possible. The reader can judge for himself how far the present research has satisfactorily done this.

More generally we have to face the issue of how far convicted defendants' perceptions of the criminal process provide one acceptable position from which that process can be examined. In the case of plea bargaining, for example, it is at least possible that what barristers, in good faith, perceive as no more than advice being offered to their clients, may be perceived by the clients themselves as pressure to change their plea. Barristers themselves may be able to accept a dual role as spokesman for the defendant and as an officer of the court, but the defendants may not find this duality easy to understand or accept. If we grant possibilities such as these then it becomes essential that researchers find some means of taking defendants' perceptions into account. The purpose of such research is not to challenge barristers' accounts of the criminal process by pitting them against those of defendants, except in the unlikely event of there being evidence of malpractice.

Both sides may be perfectly sincere in their beliefs. The purpose rather is to examine how far actions sincerely carried out in the belief that they are the most likely to produce formal justice, may unintentionally produce actual or perceived substantive injustice.

This latter point can perhaps stand as illustrative of how the growing field of socio-legal research may justify itself against the kind of attacks made on the present work. The tension between formal and substantive justice is after all a central problem for any legal system. Its importance for all members of civil society means that no one group, be they researchers or lawyers, have any prerogative in deciding the issue. What research can do is attempt to clarify the issue, and make its dimensions more clearly known, so that all members of society may be involved in the decision. Therefore, both in terms of its findings and insights and by raising these broader general issues, this research contributes to the cause of justice in our society and thereby serves the public interest.

C. M. Campbell
Paul Wiles

ACKNOWLEDGMENTS

The research discussed in this book represents part of a larger study primarily concerned with examining the outcome of jury trials in the Birmingham Crown Court. In the course of conducting the research on jury trials, it became apparent that large numbers of defendants whom we had confidently expected would plead not guilty appeared, almost literally at the last minute, to change their minds and pleaded guilty. As soon as we began to examine a few of these cases, we discovered that the explanations given to us for late changes of plea were so important that we decided to conduct an enquiry specifically relating to such cases. In this book we present the results of this enquiry and we shall publish separately the findings relating to the main study of jury trials in due course.

The research, which has been conducted under the auspices of the Institute of Judicial Administration, has been proceeding for some three years during which time we have been increasingly indebted to a large number of people. Our first debt is to the Home Office, who generously funded the entire project. Our friend and colleague, Gordon Borrie (now Director General of the Office of Fair Trading), has been a continual source of encouragement and has unselfishly given us his time despite heavy commitments as Director of the Institute of Judicial Administration and later as Dean of the Law Faculty of Birmingham University.

We also owe an enormous debt to the two Research Fellows who have been employed in the research, Kathlyn Bristow and Ann Keith, upon whose efforts the success of the field-work has in large part depended. Much of their work has involved the interviewing of elusive defendants which has necessitated visits to remote parts of the West Midlands in the evenings and at week-ends. In this work they were ably supported at various times by Graham Fridd, Jon Mallard, Tony Clark and Penny Hewson. In addition, Mr A. F. Wilcox and Dr J. P. Wilson have scrutinised for us over a thousand sets of Committal papers with the greatest thoroughness and rigour.

We have enjoyed the considerable benefit of the advice of a distinguished Consultative Committee whose members have, both individually and as a group, helped us. Mr I. S. Manson, Chief Prosecuting Solicitor of the West Midlands, Mrs Sarah McCabe and Professors W. R. Cornish, B. Z. Beinart and W. E. Cavenagh have also suggested many helpful amendments to early drafts of the manuscript.

Special mention must be made of Sergeant Stuart Harris of the West Midlands Police who has, with the greatest efficiency, carried out the onerous task of acting as our liason officer with the police. He has borne the enormous work-load involved uncomplainingly and readily answered the queries about which we have contacted him virtually daily over the past two years.

We could not have wished for a more efficient, genial and intelligent secretary than Ann Nicholas. Her untiring efforts have frequently rescued the project from disaster in times of crisis.

Our final thanks must go to our wives, Fiona and Sonia, who have adapted to our preoccupation with negotiated justice with a tolerance we had no right to expect.

The views expressed in this book are, needless to say, ours alone and are not to be taken as the views of the Home Office, members of the Consultative Committee or anyone else to whom we are indebted.

John Baldwin
Michael McConville
Birmingham 1977

FOREWORD

I am taking the unusual step of contributing a foreword to a book written by two authors within my university, and some explanation of this action is necessary.

During the past few months there has been a great deal of speculation and comment in the public press over a piece of research work done in the Institute of Judicial Administration of this university. I was concerned about the nature of some of the criticisms, particularly those that seem to reflect on the academic integrity of the authors. I wanted to determine whether or not the work had been conducted by methods which are generally accepted in the academic field and was therefore sound and the conclusions valid. I suggested to the authors that they should pay heed to the public and private comments which had been made and take advice from senior members of their discipline. They therefore briefly delayed publication to consult as widely as possible and to allow an independent academic assessment.

This was conducted by Professor Owen Hood Phillips, Emeritus Barber Professor of Jurisprudence; Professor G. E. R. Burroughs, Emeritus Professor of Education and an expert on conducting this type of research work and Professor Winifred Cavenagh, Emeritus Professor of Social Administration and Criminology, who is widely experienced in the Court. After considering the matter, they communicated with me and said: 'We consider the present work to be academically respectable. The conclusions are reasonably drawn from the evidence, so far as one can judge from the manuscript alone. Other people might have carried out a different study, used different methods and perhaps reached different conclusions; but this does not invalidate the present work. The authors have shown that there is a problem need-ing further investigation. They would not claim to have written the last word.'

Sir Robert Hunter
Vice-Chancellor, University of Birmingham

July 1977

1 BACKGROUND TO THE STUDY

Half a century ago, Raymond Moley in an article entitled 'The Vanishing Jury' observed that, though juries in the United States dealt with some of the most striking criminal cases, nonetheless the importance of the jury system was very much overshadowed by the vastly greater number of cases in which the jury was circumvented by some bargained or compromised verdict determined out of court. In England today, despite the concern expressed in some quarters about the increasing number of cases being tried by jury,[1] not only is the proportion of indictable criminal cases that comes before a jury in fact extremely small, but the proportion of guilty pleas has remained remarkably high over the past few years and there are indications that jury trials, in some areas of the country, are diminishing in number. This trend is of great legal and sociological significance, yet the reasons behind it remain largely unexplored. There is no way of ascertaining, for instance, how many of those defendants who each year plead guilty to criminal charges have been involved in some kind of bargain with the prosecution and the research evidence on the question is, to say the least, modest.

It is interesting to compare this situation with that found in the United States. Whereas the whole question of guilty plea negotiation has been largely ignored by legal writers and researchers in England, it has been a virtual obsession with American authors. Numerous books have been written on the subject and legal journals have for decades been filled with articles concerned with this topic. The question of plea bargaining,[2] which is the central concern of these writers, has now been written about to such a degree that the literature has become characterised by repetitiousness and even sterility. It is clear from this literature that in the United States the practice of bargaining for a guilty plea is now widespread, almost routine, in most jurisdictions and it is often said that, without plea bargaining, the administration of criminal justice there would break down. The variety of interests served by this covert negotiation has been extensively described[3] and, though several commentators have been concerned to indicate the very real dangers inherent in the practice of plea bargaining[4] (not least the possible conviction of the innocent), nevertheless the majority view has been in recent years that such bargaining has become an intrinsic, an inevitable, and even a desirable aspect of the judicial process that, with appropriate controls and safeguards, operates to the benefit of the equitable administration of justice, rather than to its detriment.

It is surprising, then, in view of the broad correspondence between England and the United States in the proportion of defendants who plead guilty at trial, that so few English writers have expressed an interest in the general question of guilty plea determination. Those who have written on the issues raised by plea bargaining[5] have, in general, been compelled to conduct the discussion without the support of empirical evidence, and such empirical evidence as exists is by no means definitive. Purves (1971), for example, concluded that late changes of plea, the majority of which were pleas to a lesser charge in the indictment, represented a realistic approach by police, lawyers, judges and, often, the defendants themselves.[6] Indeed, he argues further that the plea bargaining process in England in general assists the administration of justice 'without either prejudicing the rights of innocent men or occasioning real injustice to the guilty'. It is not clear, however, whether this conclusion is in fact justified by the research that was conducted. It may perhaps be the case that defendants are not prejudiced by plea bargaining and have entered into plea negotiations with a tactical awareness and spirit of realism, but it hardly seems proper to make such an assertion without first obtaining the views of the defendants in question.[7]

2

Because of the paucity of empirical research on plea determination in England, we decided, in the course of a study primarily concerned with the outcome of contested trials in the Birmingham Crown Court, to examine also the cases of a number of defendants who, having initially expressed an intention to plead not guilty, subsequently changed their plea to guilty, very often only on the day of the trial itself and commonly to a lesser count in the indictment.[8] Altogether 150 defendants fell into the late change of plea sample, these representing ten per cent of the guilty pleas that were entered in the Birmingham Crown Court in the fifteen-month period. To what extent this sample is characteristic of the mass of individuals who plead guilty at trial cannot be stated with certainty. We do not know how far the sorts of experiences we describe in relation to the narrow sample discussed in this book are common to other groups of defendants, though we have found certain parallels between their experiences and those of some of the defendants involved in other cases within our larger study of contested trials to which we shall refer later in this book. Furthermore, in a related study of defendants who pleaded guilty in the Birmingham Crown Court having themselves elected to be tried in the Crown Court,[9] comparable findings have emerged. Therefore, although it is not possible to be precise in quantitative terms, it is clear that the sorts of experiences related by the group of defendants described in this book are by no means confined to them. We cannot say how far the picture we present applies to other Crown Court centres. It may be that the experiences of defendants in Birmingham are somewhat different from those elsewhere, and, interestingly, the *Statistics on Judicial Administration*, published annually by the Lord Chancellor's Department, show that the proportion of defendants who plead guilty in the Birmingham Crown Court is higher than at any other Crown Court centre listed. The figures for 1973 and 1974 show that no fewer than 70 per cent of defendants in Birmingham pleaded guilty at the Crown Court, a figure considerably higher than the national average.

Our interest in this group of defendants arose out of an

attempt to identify, in advance of trial, those cases that would ultimately be tried by jury as part of our study of contested trials in the Birmingham Crown Court. We had noticed that very many cases that we had anticipated would be contested had, according to court staff and the police, 'folded' at the last minute. We also found that staff at the Crown Court, who assisted us in identifying likely contested cases, were more successful in this than we were but were nonetheless wrong more often than they were right.[10] We therefore decided to interview a sample of defendants to find out why so many of them changed their decision about plea so abruptly. Of 150 defendants who fell into this sample within a fifteen-month period in 1975 and 1976, we succeeded in interviewing 121 (81 per cent), though in many cases only after repeated visits to a defendant's home.[11] Obtaining a high response rate is obviously critical in research of this kind and considerable efforts were made to trace the more elusive defendants. Those who were interviewed formed a representative cross-section of the 150 individuals initially contacted in terms of age, sex, number of previous convictions and degree of suspected criminal involvement. The only significant respect in which they differed was according to the sentence they received—not surprisingly perhaps, those given custodial sentences were more likely to agree to be interviewed (95 per cent) than those who received non-custodial sentences (71 per cent). Even in the latter category, however, only 10 out of 87 individuals actually refused to be interviewed—the remaining 16 being untraceable or unable to speak English. There is no doubt, therefore, given the high response rate for all groups, that those defendants interviewed are representative of the sample as a whole.

Turning briefly to the defendants within the sample, it is important to note at the outset that they are defendants at the serious end of the crime continuum. Indeed, in five cases out of six, the reason the case was tried at the Crown Court in the first place was that either it was of such a nature that it could not be tried summarily or else the prosecution ap-

4

plied for Crown Court trial. In other words, in only a sixth of these cases did the defendant himself choose Crown Court trial. This fact is reflected in the kinds of offence with which they were charged. Four out of ten pleaded guilty to offences against the person and in some cases these were extremely serious violent or sexual assaults, which in three cases resulted in the death of the victim. The relatively serious nature of the charges to which these defendants pleaded guilty, together with the fact that no fewer than 79 per cent of them had been previously convicted of indictable criminal offences, is reflected in the sentences they were given by the court. Some 42 per cent received custodial sentences and a further 25 per cent suspended prison sentences. Only a small number were seen by the police as calculating, professional criminals—the great majority (almost three-quarters) were not suspected by the police of making much of a living out of criminal enterprises or of being much involved in any form of serious criminal activity. Most of them were in fact viewed by the police by and large as relatively unskilled, ignorant and singularly un-professional.

The interview schedule, which was fairly loosely structured, sought details of the offence with which the defendant was charged; of encounters with the police and solicitors at different stages of the penal process; of reasons for pleading guilty and of the advice received from legal advisers and others in making this decision; of the degree of satisfaction with the standard of justice received from the various parties with whom the defendant had come into contact since the time of his arrest. Finally an attempt was made to gauge the extent to which individuals suffered personal, family or social consequences as a direct result of being convicted of the offences in question. Most interviews were conducted within a month of the conclusion of the trial, although an effort was made to 'allow the dust to settle' for a week or two before making any approach in order to obtain a more considered and balanced view. Interviews were of variable length—the shortest being of perhaps only half an hour in duration, the longest well in excess of two hours. Most of the interviews were tape-

5

recorded and subsequently transcribed at length and in this book we shall use some of the qualitative material thus obtained in an attempt to convey the 'flavour' of the interviews—to appreciate, as it were, in a more incisive way than can be conveyed by mere statistical tables, the experiences of these defendants.[12] It is important to note that, as far as possible, all respondents were asked to tell their own story in response to a series of simple and neutral questions. All interviewers played very much a passive role though it was frequently necessary to tackle a respondent about apparent inconsistencies in his account of what took place or to probe for clarification on some point. There was, for instance, no mention whatever in the interview schedule, used by all interviewers, of terms such as bargain or negotiation and, where these were mentioned in the course of an interview, they arose invariably from the defendants' spontaneous accounts of their experiences. In fact, most of the information about determination of plea was elicited by means of the simple questions: 'Did you receive any advice about your plea from the police; your solicitor; your barrister; family or friends; or from anyone else?' If there was an affirmative answer to any of these questions, the defendant was then simply asked, 'What was said to you?'

It soon became apparent in the course of these interviews that the picture emerging from the available literature did not in any way correspond to the defendants' experiences as they described them to us. There seemed to have been no real attempt by recent writers to describe pressures brought to bear on defendants who wish to contest their case before a jury[13] nor any recognition of the nature of the process that many defendants undergo from the time they are first arrested by the police until their final court appearance. The interviews conducted with these defendants in Birmingham indicate an extraordinary diversity of negotiations surrounding plea, which encompass not only bargains of a give-and-take nature but also, and more importantly, the use of inducements, pressures of an extreme kind and, as the defendants see it, even moral blackmail. Far from finding that the recent judicial pronouncements[14] have reduced the extent of bargaining over plea to insignificant proportions, it appeared to us from the interviews conducted that in many cases they may even have provided defence counsel with what amounts almost to a licence to pressurise defendants into pleading guilty. The outcome produced by out-of-court negotiation appears to us to have been unjust for many defendants in the sample.

We shall be concerned to explore the parallels that exist between the kinds of pressures that defendants in this sample describe and those that have been described in the comprehensive American literature on the subject. As noted above, earlier work in England has tended to minimise the importance of pre-trial negotiation as a feature of the criminal process here and various writers have suggested that, insofar as such negotiation does occur, it represents a solution that serves well the interests of all concerned and is likely adequately to reflect the true involvement of the defendant in the offence charged.[15] We shall question each of these statements —indeed, we shall argue that the established practice of allowing some reduction of sentence in return for a plea of guilty has allowed a situation to arise (and in one sense may be seen to have created it) in which unfair pressures have been placed upon defendants to plead guilty. We shall also examine those cases involving defendants who stridently maintain their innocence but who say they were persuaded by their lawyers to plead guilty, though often under protest. In this discussion, our concern is not to describe those minor dysfunctions that are inevitable in any system of administering justice: we refer to injustices that seem endemic in any system that allows a substantial sentencing discount for a guilty plea. For some of our cases we shall argue that there was a miscarriage of justice, and if we are right about this and if our sample of cases in Birmingham is not wholly unrepresentative of the country at large, it would appear that earlier estimates of the numbers of people wrongly convicted and imprisoned are likely considerably to underestimate the real figure.

We shall at various points in this book be critical of practices of many of the individuals with whom the defendants

7

came into contact, and particularly critical of certain members of the Bar. In fairness to the Bar, we should state at the outset that, though many of the practices we describe constitute in our view unprofessional conduct, we do not suggest by any means that more than a small minority of barristers involved in our sample of cases behaved in this way.[16] Our allegations of unfair or coercive conduct relate to only a small number of cases and in the remainder it appeared to us that counsel acted properly. It is appropriate to state explicitly that the primary objective of this book is not to castigate the Bar as a whole nor even to impugn the conduct of individual barristers but rather to raise more fundamental questions about a system that encourages, and lends legitimacy to, many of the doubtful practices that we shall describe in subsequent chapters. It remains the case, however, that we shall be critical at many points of the conduct of individual barristers on the basis of what defendants have said to us without having the benefit of the barrister's side of the story. It should be pointed out that we did approach the Bar in July 1974 with a view to obtaining their co-operation in our main research on contested cases. However, we formed the view, as a result of the nature of their response to that approach, that it would not be worthwhile seeking their co-operation in relation to the present sample of cases. The Bar's principal objection to participating in the research on contested trials was that to do so would breach the obligation of confidentiality to the client. As they put it: 'Counsel has a duty of confidence to his client. This is an obligation of the most imperative character and no relaxation is possible save with the consent of the client.' There were, however, in the view of the Bar, formidable problems in relation to obtaining a full and satisfactory consent from the client. In the result, the Bar expressed the view that it could assist only by 'supplying factual information strictly confined to matters of public record and which occurred in open Court'. Moreover, we submitted to the Bar, in the summer of 1974, various draft questionnaires that included questions relating to change of plea cases. But we were told

8

that 'there is no way in which this question can be answered without a breach of privilege'. In the light of these responses from the Bar, we could see no purpose whatever in requesting their co-operation in relation to the present study, since any meaningful interview with counsel would inevitably have infringed this basic obligation of confidentiality.[17]

Much of the information upon which this study is based then is drawn from the interviews conducted with defendants —all indeed now convicted criminals. This immediately raises the difficulty—and it would be foolish to deny its importance —that such individuals may well deliberately lie about certain aspects of their cases; alternatively, they may be genuinely confused about what happened and unwittingly mislead an interviewer, or else they may in a great variety of different ways exaggerate or minimise detailed aspects of their cases that seem to them particularly important or insignificant. That many defendants, consciously or unconsciously, distorted their stories in these ways when they spoke to us is beyond question. Whether this means that their accounts of what took place can, or should, therefore, be dismissed is much more doubtful. We are firmly of the view that they should not. It has been put to us—and it is appropriate that we should give our response before discussing what the defendants said to us—that we are merely reporting the sort of criticisms that are typically voiced by any sample of convicted criminals. The answer to this is that it is simply not true and, having interviewed almost 500 defendants, we can say with certainty that the comments of those who changed plea at a late stage are, in very many important respects, different from those customarily encountered. A comparison of their responses, for instance, with those of over 350 defendants in our main sample of contested cases (over half of whom were convicted criminals in the same sense) indicates that the late plea changers are as a group more critical of the legal process they have experienced and have stronger views on the subject; they are much more critical of their own barrister and report far more often a feeling of non-involvement in their trial and what immediately preceded it. In short, they are as a group much more angry, confused and alienated than any other group of defendants we have ourselves examined and, as far as we are aware, any other researcher in England has examined.

Having said this, it remains the case that we are heavily dependent on what the defendants themselves said to us,[18] and throughout the field-work we have been conscious of the limitations that this imposes. There are several important points that should be borne in mind in evaluating the veracity of the defendants' stories. In the first place, defendants were given no prior warning, beyond in some cases a bland introductory letter, of the purpose of the interview. It would in consequence have been extremely difficult for them—and have served no real purpose—to concoct a spurious account of their case and to have maintained the pretence successfully throughout a long and testing interview. Secondly, the main thrust of the questions in the interviews was concerned less with the facts relating to the offence than with details of their court appearance and the events immediately preceding it. It might be expected that some defendants would wish to lie about their alleged involvement in an offence (although in many of our cases the defendant openly admitted his guilt), if only to maintain a story consistent with that given at court, but it is less likely that a defendant would lie about matters that were never even raised at the court hearing. Thirdly, as will be clear from the body of this book, it would be wrong to dismiss the stories that defendants tell on the basis that they are simply the victims of the criminal process who are getting their own back on the system. The defendants almost without exception discriminated carefully between the various people who dealt with their cases; all those whom the defendants encountered from arrest to sentence were separately assessed. Moreover, many defendants in the sample did not see themselves as victims of the system at all, having received a tangible and acceptable benefit from a bargain, or having been co-opted into the out-of-court negotiation process to such an extent that they saw no injustice in being subjected to pressures, even of a coercive nature. Furthermore, in a small group of cases, the defendant's story was corrobor-
10

ated by that of a co-defendant interviewed separately, there having been no opportunity for them to invent a common story. In some of these cases, the defendants had not spoken to each other after their appearance in court because, for example, only one had been given a custodial sentence. In several cases, the defendants in question had been represented by a single barrister and the detailed accounts they gave of the pre-trial advice they had been given on plea tallied in every material respect. When evidence was available from alternative sources (e.g. solicitors, police officers), this never reduced our confidence in a defendant's story and, in important respects, often strengthened it.

Whether or not these statements by defendants are accepted as valid, however, the more important point, in our view, is that they reflect the defendants' experiences as *they* understood and perceived them. For instance, where defendants say they have been 'forced' to plead guilty by their barrister, this interpretation of the encounter is more significant than whether the conduct of the barrister in question was in fact outside the strict ethical rules governing the advice that can be given in this regard. As we have already argued, there seems to us good reason to think that, in many cases, defendants' stories of what took place are highly credible, but it is their interpretation of what took place that is critical in understanding their decision to plead guilty. To take one example: where a defendant pleads guilty because he has been advised that on conviction following a not guilty plea he is likely to receive twelve years' imprisonment, but only half that if he pleads guilty (the sort of advice that has been sanctioned by the Court of Appeal), the fact that the advice was merely advice, and proper advice at that, may well be of secondary importance in understanding his decision if the defendant believes that the alternatives put to him by his barrister are ones that will *certainly* follow. In other words, it is our contention that the defendant's subjective experience is more crucial in this respect than the objective reality. It is primarily with these subjective experiences that we shall be concerned in this book.

As other researchers have found, there is no typical defenddant. The defendants in our sample are highly diverse—from the hardened recidivist in the prison to the bewildered housewife. Our sample includes unemployed labourers, sales representatives, soldiers, students, housewives and even a lawyer.[19] As we shall indicate later in this book, there are several cases in our separate sample of contested cases in which acquitted defendants describe pressures of a similar nature being brought to bear even on them. Some of these defendants are now accepted by the police to have been quite innocent of the charges they faced and to have been rightly acquitted. It is not the case, therefore, that the experiences we shall describe are those of guilty men only; indeed, as will become apparent, it is truer to say that the experiences are those of the compliant as well as those of the guilty. Finally, all those involved in the interviewing of these defendants[20] are firmly of the view that the great majority of respondents were being truthful about those details of their cases material to our enquiry. It is our considered view that, though interviews with defendants will not by any means provide a full or wholly accurate picture of all the circumstances surrounding the decision to plead guilty, they nonetheless raise questions about a greatly neglected aspect of the administration of justice in England.

We are ourselves convinced of the value of obtaining the defendant's story of what took place. Whether their views are sufficiently reliable to support our contention that the pressures to plead guilty that were brought to bear on certain defendants can only reflect ill on the legal system is, in the final analysis, very much a matter of personal judgment. Although we make this important caveat, we can see no other satisfactory way of approaching the question of guilty plea negotiation than through the defendant himself. Since all informal discussions of this nature are, almost by definition, conducted in camera, formal observation is not possible.

Though the views of defendants represent the main focus of attention in this study, they were not the only sources of information available about these cases. We obtained from the Birmingham Crown Court copies of all the committal

12

papers (statements and depositions)[21] relating to our sample of cases and had these examined independently by two highly experienced individuals—one a retired Chief Constable, the other a retired Justices' Clerk.[22] They were asked to make a prediction of the likely outcome of each case on the assumption that the case would be contested and also to specify the degree of certainty (on a five-point scale) with which they made the prediction. In none of the cases was this prediction made with any knowledge of what happened at the trial and as far as possible committal papers were sent to them in advance of trial for all cases that appeared likely to be contested.[23] The main value of these independent assessments for this group of cases is that it provided the informed views from two experts who were basing their predictions essentially on as much of the prosecution's case as defence counsel had to hand in advising his client on plea.

As indicated above, we also obtained a good deal of information about each defendant from the police. In addition to providing details of any previous criminal convictions (and acquittals), the police supplied details of the *suspected* involvement of defendants in serious criminal activity that had not been the subject of criminal prosecution. Details of this nature have not, as far as we are aware, been made available before to researchers in England and they provide several measurements of what is loosely termed 'professional' criminal activity. The West Midlands Police not only provided information on the known and suspected involvement of defendants in serious crime, but individual officers also gave their opinions on the level of skill demonstrated by each defendant in his criminal activities; his suspected involvement in 'organised' crime (i.e. crime involving gangs, planning, use of equipment, etc.); the extent to which a defendant was suspected of making a living out of crime and, finally, the extent to which he was aware of his legal rights and prepared to resort even to illegal means to avoid conviction. Each of these measures taps well-established (though not necessarily related) indices of what is popularly known as 'professional' crime. Though they can be only crudely defined and arbitrarily measured, we

13

do nonetheless think that they provide (particularly when aggregated into an overall measure) a more accurate reflection of professionalism than any used earlier by other researchers and certainly one that is more adequate than the commonly used index of previous criminal record.[24]

These measures of professionalism provided an opportunity of testing the hypothesis, implicit in the work particularly of Newman (1956) and Chambliss (1969), that certain groups of defendants (specifically professional crooks and other types of sophisticated and experienced criminals) are able to secure much greater benefits and concessions from informal pre-trial negotiations than their more gullible and naïve counterparts. Chambliss, for example, states this proposition in the following direct way:

> ... the professional criminal can offer the system compensations for leniency and is therefore in a much stronger bargaining position than the amateur or occasional thief. It would therefore seem likely that we would typically fill our corrective institutions ... with a predominantly youthful, quasi-criminal group while the more systematic and sophisticated offenders would be relatively unimpaired by the law. [p. 209]

We shall be concerned to test this hypothesis, and others, in the course of this report and shall draw extensively upon available American literature in so far as it includes discussion of issues common to England. It is our contention that the whole question of plea determination in England has been greatly misunderstood by many writers and we shall, in the chapters that follow, question many of the assumptions they have made in this respect. In short, we do not accept, at least as uncritically as others have accepted, that within this broad area there is any necessary correspondence between the 'law in action' and the 'law in books'.

NOTES AND REFERENCES

1. See, for instance, the discussion in the Report of the Interdepartmental Committee (under the chairmanship of Lord Justice James) *The Distribution of Criminal Business between the Crown Court and the Magistrates' Court* (1975) Cmnd. 6323.

2. The meaning of the term is discussed in chapter 2. It is used, in the words of Jackson (1972), to describe 'an informal agreement that the defendant will plead guilty to a particular offence in return for a promise that he will not be prosecuted for a more serious offence, or if he is already charged with the more serious offence that his plea of not guilty will be accepted, or simply that he will receive a lighter sentence than if he fights the case' (p. 208).

3. See particularly on this Miller (1927); Enker (1967); Fay (1968); *University of Richmond Law Review* (1972); Smith and Dale (1973); Wheatley (1974).

4. The most important critics include Moley (1928); Dash (1951); Sudnow (1965); Blumberg (1967); Rosett (1967); Whitman (1967); Alschuler (1968, 1975); Casper (1972); Dean (1974).

5. See, P. Thomas (1969, 1970); Davis (1971); Adams (1971); Heberling (1973).

6. See also the supporting evidence in McCabe and Purves (1972a).

7. See, Purves (1971) p. 472: 'This is not merely an impression gleaned from the demeanour of defendants: it is a hard fact that as high a proportion as 79.4 per cent of all defendants who changed their pleas at this late stage had previous convictions recorded against them, and it might not be too bold to assume that some, if not many, of the remaining 20.6 per cent would have had either acquittals or previous contact with the police, the law, or the courts.' This reasoning, particularly in view of the American evidence that recidivists may well be especially at risk in the bargaining process, needs qualification.

8. The defendants in the sample fell into two broad groups. First those who, faced with several counts in an indictment, had their plea of not guilty to the more serious count accepted by the court, having pleaded guilty to a lesser count; and secondly, those who pleaded guilty at or immediately before trial. Most defendants in the sample qualified for inclusion on both grounds (i.e. they had changed their plea to a lesser count at the last moment).

9. This research is being conducted for a doctoral dissertation by Mr A. D. Clark.

10. McCabe and Purves (1972a), who were engaged on a similar study of verdicts, encountered the same difficulties and undertook a separate study of 170 cases in which defendants 'by-passed' the jury. This study included 58 cases in which an acquittal was ordered or directed by the judge.

11. We would like to record our gratitude to the authorities at Winson

Green Prison and at several other prisons, borstals and detention centres for kindly making available to us facilities for interviewing defendants who received custodial sentences.

12. It was suggested by colleagues that the tape-recording of interviews problems because it makes respondents inhibited (see also Bottoms and McClean, 1976, p. 15). Our experience, which now covers over 1,000 recorded interviews, indicates that in the vast majority of cases defendants rapidly become indifferent to the tape-recorder and spoke without undue suspicion or reserve. An additional advantage of using tape-recorders was that we were ourselves able to play back all recordings to satisfy ourselves that no variations in interviewing style or transcription distorted the results.

13. One possible exception to this is the recently published study by Bottoms and McClean (1976), though their research primarily focuses on defendants who are tried in the Magistrates' Courts.

14. The case law on this is discussed in chapters 2 and 3.

15. Purves (1971); Davis (1971).

16. Only four Queen's Counsel were involved in our total sample of cases and all the allegations of unprofessional conduct relate to less experienced barristers.

17. After a draft of this book was sent to the Bar in 1976, the Bar suggested that we offer all barristers involved the opportunity to comment on the defendants' statements. We were unable to take up this offer because it would have necessitated breaking guarantees of confidentiality that had been given to all defendants interviewed. Moreover, we ourselves were doubtful of the value of interviewing barristers about these cases, all of which had been concluded at least eight months previously. We raised the question at a meeting of our Consultative Committee and it was there agreed that this would be a pointless exercise. Another suggestion was that we examine the briefs relating to these cases in order to compare the statements given by the defendants to their solicitors with the statements made during the course of the interviews with us. Once again, however, it was not possible to do this without revealing the identities of the defendants concerned. In February 1977 we offered the Bar an opportunity to contribute a statement to be included in this book. For reasons that have not been communicated to us, the Bar rejected this offer.

18. Similar exercies have been undertaken, though often for quite different purposes, by other researchers. See, particularly, Newman (1956); Casper (1972); Martin and Webster (1971); Bottoms and McClean (1976); Arcuri (1976).

19. In all cases mentioned in the text, we have disguised any detail that might identify any individual concerned.

20. Over a quarter of the interviews were conducted by the present writers, the remainder being done by two full-time research fellows (both qualified social workers), by a postgraduate student conducting his own research in a related area, and by two individuals seconded from Birmingham Polytechnic on a full-time basis for a one year period for the purpose of research assistance.

21. Committal papers, which are made available to all parties prior to each trial, represent in essence the prosecution case.
22. The two men concerned are Mr A. F. Wilcox, C.B.E., Q.P.M. (formerly Chief Constable of Hertfordshire) and Dr J. P. Wilson, O.B.E. (formerly Clerk to the Sunderland Justices and an editor of Stone's Justices' Manual between 1952 and 1968).
23. In all, well in excess of 1,000 different sets of committal papers were sent during the course of the research to the predictors to examine. Most of these papers related to the outcome of cases likely to be contested, as part of our study of jury trials. As far as was possible, predictions were obtained prospectively.
24. See, for instance, Zander (1974); Baldwin and McConville (1974); Mack (1976). The aggregated measure of professionalism adopted in this study is not significantly correlated for the 150 defendants in the sample with the number of previous criminal convictions.

2 PLEA BARGAINING IN THE BIRMINGHAM CROWN COURT

If plea bargaining exists in England, it has certainly been well hidden from researchers. Most researchers and commentators in England accept that, whilst there may be some limited pressures upon a defendant to plead guilty to an offence, there is little scope for bargains to be struck over plea. Since we wish to discriminate, in discussing our sample of defendants, between the several kinds of consideration a defendant may have to take into account when determining his plea, we shall confine the term 'plea bargain' to its settled usage.

'Plea bargaining' is not a term of art, but it has now acquired a generally accepted meaning. Generally speaking, a bargained plea in the United States involves some arrangement between the prosecutor and the defence whereby the prosecutor agrees to make some concession in return for which the defendant agrees to enter a mutually acceptable guilty plea. The concession made by the prosecutor may take one of a number of forms.[1] Professor Newman (1956), a leading American commentator on plea bargaining, found in his study in Wisconsin that the considerations received by defendants in exchange for their guilty pleas were of four general types: (i) sentence concessions (45 per cent of his sample) where, for example, a non-custodial sentence might be held out instead of imprisonment; (ii) concurrent pressing of multiple charges (22 per cent); (iii) reductions of the charge from the one alleged in the complaint (20 per cent); (iv) dropping one or more charges (13 per cent). The common nexus between these forms of bargains is

18

that they are all intended to get the defendant a lighter sentence. As Davis (1971) puts it:

> The defendant may get a promise of a sentence recommendation, or a reduction of the charges against him, or a dismissal of some charges; but the linking factor between these elements is that their effect—or supposed effect—from the defendant's point of view, is on the sentence which will be passed on him as a result of his plea of guilty. The reduction or dismissal of charges as part of a plea agreement is merely a less direct way of affecting sentence than having the prosecution make recommendations on the subject to the court (as it can in most of the United States' jurisdictions). [p. 151]

Plea bargaining, then, describes the practice whereby the defendant enters a plea of guilty in return for which he will be given some consideration that results in a sentence concession.

The guilty plea has become a crucial factor in the administration of criminal justice in the United States. It is commonly said that up to ninety per cent of all criminal prosecutions in the United States result in guilty pleas.[2] How many of these guilty pleas are a result of bargaining is not known, but the available research evidence suggests that a majority of guilty pleas follow upon some informal negotiation between the prosecution and the defence. In a survey of 97 men convicted of felonies in Wisconsin, for example, Newman (1956) found that 94 per cent had pleaded guilty and that over half of these claimed that they had bargained for their sentences.[3] Other studies have generally confirmed Newman's findings.[4] In the United States, therefore, the vast majority of convictions in criminal cases are the result of a plea of guilty and most of these pleas are apparently arrived at following informal discussions between the defence and the prosecutor in which some inducement to plead guilty is sought by the defence and obtained from the prosecutor. The general view of commentators is that, whatever may be the position in the United States, in England there is far less scope for such plea arrangements.[5] It is easy to find good reasons why the incidence of bargains is lower in England than in the United States; they relate to differences in the sentencing system, the role of the prosecution, the judicial supervision over the charge, and the legal restrictions on the involvement of the judge in any bargain discussions.

In discussing the extent of plea bargaining, commentators have noted important differences in the extent to which trial judges in England and the United States have been able to retain their sentencing discretion.[6] In England, only murder carries a mandatory sentence, so that the essential characteristics of the sentencing process are discretion and flexibility reposing in the judge. In the United States, on the other hand, numerous offences in many jurisdictions carry mandatory sentences, some of an extreme nature. These differences are likely to affect the extent of plea bargaining in at least two ways. In the first place, the sentencing discretion of the judge in England would appear to make any bargaining between the prosecution and defence over sentence redundant. Even if, for example, the prosecution felt that a sentence of imprisonment was not merited in a particular case, no guarantees could be given to the defence on sentence as this is a matter wholly within the judge's discretion. Whilst it is common in the United States for the prosecutor to promise to recommend to the court a particular sentence, an undertaking of this nature cannot properly be given in England where a specific sentence recommendation by prosecution counsel would be unethical.[7] In the second place, the severe minimum sentences imposed by penal statutes in many parts of the United States give an impetus to informal procedures that have the effect of mitigating the harshness of the law. There is, therefore, an additional pressure for the use of plea bargaining in the United States that is not present in this country. This is in some part borne out by Newman's study. He found that Wisconsin was characterised by straight guilty pleas to the charges as they stood ('on-the-nose' pleas), whereas both Kansas and Michigan were notable for their reliance on negotiated pleas of guilty to reduced charges. The explanation for this was to be found in the differences in sentencing structures of the states:

Both Michigan and Kansas are characterized by legislatively fixed sentences, which seriously limit judicial discretion in sentencing; whereas Wisconsin law provides low minima for virtually all crimes, discretion of the court to fix the maximum term within legislative limits, and probation as an alternative to incarceration for all offences. [Newman, 1966, p. 54]

A second factor relevant to the incidence of plea bargaining is the different nature of the prosecution systems in the two countries.[8] In the United States, the prosecutor is a paid official who exercises a largely unfettered discretion. In a great many circumstances, it is the prosecutor who is able to determine the outcome of a case. Many jurisdictions require the agreement of the trial judge to any charge reduction and some states additionally require the prosecutor to file a statement with the court disclosing the reasons for the charge reduction. In practice, however, as La Fave writes:[9]

> ... judicial control is minimal; the judge typically accepts the lesser plea without question, and the prosecutor's explanation (if required by law or practice) is usually no more explicit than 'in the interests of justice'. [1970, p. 540]

This is supported by the early report of Weintraub and Tough (1942) who examined the ruling that the District Attorney should give a written account explaining why he accepted a plea of guilty to a lesser charge. They found that the reasons given fell generally into a distinct pattern—generalised in nature—'second offender', 'punishment is sufficient', and the like. All this is in marked contrast to the English system, where criminal prosecutions are not usually conducted by professional prosecutors. In the Crown Court, prosecutions are generally conducted by barristers who commonly appear for the Crown in one case and for the defence in another. Here counsel does not have the same unregulated power to manipulate charges or to offer other inducements in order to obtain a plea of guilty. Indeed, as David Thomas (1968) has noted, it is far from clear who in England would have authority to enter into plea negotiation on behalf of the prosecution. Although it may be the case, for these and other reasons,

21

that no prosecution mentality has been able to develop in the English system,[10] it is possible that, with the growth of prosecuting solicitors' departments, there will increasingly develop such a prosecution mentality. It is still true to say, however, that the prosecutor in England does not have sufficient discretion to enable him to enter into bargaining for plea in the same way as his American counterpart.

If the prosecutor is allowed to control the nature of the charges brought, unsupervised by the courts, the scope for plea bargains is likely to be increased. For in such a situation the prosecutor, in anticipation of being able to extract a guilty plea on some count, may overcharge defendants or reduce the charge below the level justified by the facts alleged. In the United States there is in theory some control by the courts over the charge brought. Thus the Federal Rules of Criminal Procedure state that:

> Notwithstanding the acceptance of a plea of guilty, the court shall not enter a judgment upon such plea without making such inquiry as shall satisfy it that there is a factual basis for the plea.[11]

This Rule is not, however, binding upon state court judges,[12] and some courts have gone so far as to accept pleas of guilty to offences that do not exist.[13] In England, on the other hand, the courts have been insistent that the charge brought should match the facts alleged. In *Soanes*,[14] Lord Goddard C.J. said that it was the duty of counsel for the Crown, where nothing appears in the depositions that could be said to reduce the crime to some lesser offence than the one charged, to present the offence charged in the indictment, leaving it to the jury if they saw fit to find a verdict of guilty to the lesser offence only. The courts have deprecated charge reduction in the interests of convenience or as an inducement to guilty pleas and have emphasised that the over-riding consideration must always be the proper administration of criminal justice.[15] The English prosecutor is, therefore, prevented from precipitating a plea bargain by means of an undue reduction in the charge.

Many of the matters noted above would not succeed in

22

restricting bargaining over plea if the English judge was permitted to be a party to plea negotiation. At present, if the prosecution and the defence strike a bargain over sentence, there is no way in which the prosecution can guarantee that the eventual sentence will be that agreed upon. This would change if the judge was allowed to be party to the negotiations or to indicate the form and quantum of the sentence he has in mind at the bargaining stage. But it is now clear that any judicial involvement of this nature in the defendant's determination of plea will vitiate the plea of guilty. The leading case is *Turner*,[16] in which the defendant was indicted for theft and pleaded not guilty. During the course of the prosecution's case, Turner's counsel advised him in strong terms to change his plea, on the basis that on a plea of guilty he might well be awarded a non-custodial sentence, whereas if he continued with his not guilty plea he ran the risk of going to prison. Turner refused to take this advice. Counsel then went to discuss the matter with the judge, came back and repeated his earlier advice and, shortly afterwards, Turner changed his plea to guilty. Turner was fined and an order for costs made against him, but he then appealed against his conviction on the ground that his change of plea had been involuntary because of the pressure exerted on him by counsel, and because he had believed that counsel had been expressing the views of the judge. On the first point, the court took the view that counsel had not exceeded the bounds of his duty and deprived Turner of a free choice over his plea. On the second point, however, the appeal succeeded because, once it was shown that Turner felt that the views expressed emanated from the judge, it was idle to think that he really had a free choice in the matter of plea. The plea was therefore treated as a nullity, and the court ordered a proper trial. The court went on to make certain observations on judicial involvement in the determination of plea.[17] There must be freedom of access between counsel and the judge,[18] but any discussion which takes place must be between the judge and both counsel for the defence and counsel for the prosecution, and the defence solicitor should be allowed to attend if he so desires.

Such discussions may be desirable where, for example, there are matters arising of such a nature that counsel cannot, in the interests of his client, mention them in open court; but discussion should take place only when really necessary, for it is important that justice be administered in open court. The Court of Appeal was emphatic that the judge should never indicate to counsel the sentence he has in mind, unless he is able to say that, whatever the plea, the sentence will or will not take a particular form.[19] As a final observation, it was said that where a discussion does take place with the judge, defence counsel should disclose this to the accused and inform him of what took place.[20] The influence that a judge may properly bring to bear upon the defendant's decision on plea is, therefore, limited, so that one factor prompting plea bargaining in many parts of the United States[21] is missing in England.

It would appear, then, for the reasons mentioned above, that the scope for plea bargaining in England is limited, and commentators have not been slow to draw this conclusion. Thus Davis (1971) concluded his review of plea bargaining practices in America and England in the following way:

> As for England, there is no evidence of 'bargains' being transacted in any quantifiable number in the English courts. All the evidence suggests that the courts are completely intent on retaining their discretions, both as to determining the level of criminal culpability of those who come before them, and as to sentencing. [p. 228]

It is clear from our research in the Birmingham Crown Court, however, that this conclusion is not one that can be justified. Indeed, a casual visit to the Birmingham Crown Court would rapidly dispel the misconception that plea bargaining scarcely exists in English courts in other than a most rudimentary form. The observer could daily overhear barristers, police officers and others refer to the 'deals' that have been struck, the anticipated contested trials that have 'folded' or the 'carve up' of a case that is expected. He would also notice that not all parties are equally satisfied with the bargains that are made—some parties are delighted, some are

24

relieved, whilst others are decidedly disgruntled, if not angry. Many of the defendants we interviewed, and particularly the recidivists among them, regard this kind of dealing as a standard, if somewhat underhand, method of administering justice and it is to some of them a much more realistic and acceptable way of proceeding than, say, taking their chance with a jury. One of the recidivists in the sample, who was charged with wounding with intent, made the following observation about this system:

> *Case 29*: For someone without a lot of form, the police probably would have charged them with assault and have it weighed off at the Magistrates. But once you've got a lot of form, they say, 'Right, we'll go upstairs.' They use section 18 assault to frighten you and as an excuse to get you to Crown Court. Usually they'll make a deal on it—it's what they call plea bargaining ... the barrister who's defending and the one who's prosecuting have got it pretty nearly sewn up. They're in the law courts everyday and they know what's going on. They brow-beat many people [into pleading guilty]. Where they've got a long indictment, they talk between themselves like a couple of carpenters saying 'We'll cut that piece to that length.' It's just a job for them.

It is well known that the criminal courts are in large measure dependent on at least the tacit co-operation or compliance of the great majority of defendants if they are not to become overwhelmed by the sheer number of cases with which they have to deal.[22] Even a small increase in the proportion of contested trials can present enormous difficulties for the administrative organisation of the courts. There are pressures at all stages of the criminal process to induce defendants to plead guilty and the rewards for so doing are often considerable. Very few defendants resist these pressures to the bitter end. Only about three per cent of those charged with indictable offences are eventually tried by jury. Most defendants with whom we are concerned in this study resist the pressures to plead guilty until almost literally the last minute.[23] We shall explore the reasons behind this apparently inconsistent decision in the remainder of this chapter.

25

It is worth noting immediately that there are a small number of defendants, almost exclusively those experienced in court procedure, who made what was simply a strategic decision to withhold their guilty plea until such time as they were able to secure the maximum benefit from any concession that might be offered by the prosecution. In truth this small group of recidivists were attempting, not always successfully, to manipulate the legal system to serve their own ends. Most of these defendants probably had little intention of contesting the case if no offers were forthcoming.[24] Much more common than this group, however, are those defendants who, from the outset, are determined to contest the case at trial and who, frequently with the encouragement and support of their solicitor, resist what are often considerable pressures to change their plea to guilty. Then, only on the day of the trial itself, they are shocked and bewildered to find that defence counsel advises them, often in irresistibly strong language, to plead guilty. A good illustration of this pattern is provided by the following case.

> *Case 122*: The solicitor wanted me to plead not guilty all the way along until the Crown Court. He kept saying, 'You're all right, you know. When we get to the Crown Court, we'll win it.' Then, all of a sudden, for no reason at all, the barrister advised me that I might as well plead guilty. I was astounded really. I said, 'What have I come this far for if you're going to tell me to plead guilty?' In the end, I just pleaded guilty to get it over and done with really. I still am innocent but what can you do? I'd got no choice but to plead guilty—that's how I saw it anyway. If your barrister comes up to you and tells you you've got a 50–50 chance, that if you plead guilty you'll get off with less than if you plead innocent, well, what would you do?

It is important, then, to distinguish between the various forms of pressures and inducements that these defendants described and these are what we shall discuss in this and the following chapter. It is very difficult, however, to examine this question with any degree of precision particularly because, as was noted in chapter 1, any classification adopted is based on the defendant's report of what took place and, for a variety of reasons, this report may be incomplete or distorted. However, it was possible with all defendants to categorise fairly precisely their main reasons for pleading guilty. Not surprisingly, for many of the defendants in the sample there had been no attempt made to bargain or pressurise them to plead guilty. The decision to plead guilty was theirs alone and usually (though not always) it merely reflected the defendant's admitted involvement in the offence alleged. However, only 35 defendants fell within this group and it came as something of a surprise to us to find that over 70 per cent of the whole sample appeared to have been involved in some kind of 'negotiated' justice.

We distinguish here four broad categories of defendants within this sample of cases: first, those who are guilty as charged where no pressure is exerted or inducement offered; secondly, those at the opposite extreme who claim to have been involved in genuine plea bargains; thirdly, those defendants who have no accurate knowledge of any bargain struck with the judge or the prosecution but who nonetheless operate on the understanding that something has been going on 'behind the scenes' to which they are not themselves party; and finally, numerically the largest group, those who were involved in no deals or bargains of any kind but who said that they decided to plead guilty in response to advice or pressure from their own barrister.[25]

It is evident from the interviews conducted that, although there is clearly no highly organised system of plea bargaining in England (in the sense that such a system is found in many states in the United States), many defendants appeared to have been involved in plea bargains in a more complete sense than has been appreciated by many contemporary writers. These defendants were involved in plea bargains in the sense that they said that, in return for pleading guilty, their barrister had been able to strike a bargain with either the judge or the prosecution and, as a direct result of this, an offer was made to them that they had accepted. As a defence solicitor involved in one of the cases within this sample put it:

27

The fairly common practice adopted by the judge probably caused the accused here to acknowledge the truth by his plea—all the same disturbing that the accused should be put in such a position.

We shall discuss in the course of this chapter the variety of bargains that defendants described. In the following chapter, we shall examine the sorts of pressures to which many defendants said they were subject from their own lawyers. In both groups of cases, we shall argue that the defendant's freedom of choice has been in many instances impaired and in consequence the voluntariness of his plea of guilty is called into question. At this stage, it is important to note that, in terms of understanding why this sample of defendants decided to plead guilty, pressure from their own barrister is given as the most important single factor.

The following table presents the reasons given by the 121 defendants for pleading guilty:

	No.	%
No deal or pressure—defendant guilty as pleaded	35	28.9
Plea bargain—an offer made and accepted by defendant and benefit accrues to him	22	18.2
No explicit bargain but defendant thinks or assumes that a bargain struck on his behalf		
Pressure from barrister but no specific offer made to defendant	48	39.7
	121	100.0

Over one in six defendants, then, claimed to have been party to plea bargains proper. It is noticeable that this group considerably over-represents the recidivists in the sample. Almost 70 per cent had at least five previous convictions for indictable criminal offences compared with 48 per cent in the main sample. There are probably two main reasons why recidivists are involved in such bargaining. First, they 'know the ropes'; they are familiar with court procedure and court personnel and, as noted above, many anticipate that a compromise of some kind will be reached or some concession offered. Since they know that there are rewards for compliance, some defendants attempt to 'work the system' by deliberately delaying pleading guilty until the last minute. Second, and probably of greater importance, they know better than anyone that the stakes for them are high not only in terms of the heavier sentence that will be imposed if they contest the case unsuccessfully but they know that, if they wish to challenge the police evidence (and particularly the police 'verbals' which so many of them allege comprise the substance of the case against them), they run the serious risk of having their own character called into question and their criminal record revealed to the jury. In short, they know from their experience that it is often easier to cut their losses and be co-operative.

It is important to examine carefully the main kinds of bargains described by this group of plea bargainers. Interestingly, there is a good deal of consistency in the experiences they describe and in all but three of the 22 cases the plea bargain appeared to take the form of a straightforward offer regarding the sentence that would be imposed. In over half the cases, the defendant said he had been told of a specific sentence he would receive if he pleaded guilty, and sometimes warned of a quite different and heavier sentence if he continued with his plea of not guilty. In a third of the cases, the offer was apparently made only in general terms— for instance, that a man would not be sent to prison if he pleaded guilty. In the vast majority of such cases, the bargain was honoured. In only three cases did the bargain take the form of charge reduction, and in none of these cases was any offer or promise held out to the defendant about the consequent sentence to be imposed. The following examples illustrate the variety of the bargains described to us by defendants in this group of bargained cases:

> *Case 13* [specific offer to a defendant]: The barrister wanted to get it over with. He went to see the judge with the other barrister and told me that if I pleaded guilty, I

would get a suspended sentence but if I fought the case, I'd be done for wasting the court's time and would get 3 years imprisonment or, if I was lucky, a suspended sentence. He left it up to me—so I pleaded guilty and got a suspended sentence.

Case 20 [specific offer made to a youth charged initially with rape]: The barrister intimated that I should plead guilty. I was angry but he pointed one or two things out, but I still said I wanted to fight it. Then he went away and had a word with the judge. He came back and said there wasn't sufficient evidence of rape and they would alter the charge to indecent assault. He suggested that I plead guilty to that. He said we didn't want this poor girl to have to go into the witness box. I asked him if I would go to prison. He disappeared again and came back and said he'd spoken to the judge who intimated that he would fine me. He said, 'Are you agreeable to that?' I said, 'Yes, I am.'

Case 24 [a general offer]: The barrister said he didn't fancy my chances if I pleaded not guilty. He said 'If I can get the charge reduced and the judge to agree not to send you away, will you plead guilty?' He then talked to the judge and the prosecution. I agreed to plead guilty to assault. The barrister said the judge didn't actually say I wouldn't go to prison but he said 'Clearly prison is no good for this man, he needs something else.'

Case 61 [a specific offer made to a defendant charged with wounding and carrying an offensive weapon]: The solicitor and barrister were involved together. The solicitor contacted the barrister and they went to see the judge. They advised me to plead guilty to carrying an offensive weapon and I was actually given the choice of a fine or a suspended sentence. I chose the fine—I didn't like a suspended sentence hanging over my head.

Case 132 [a specific offer]: The trial went on for a week. The judge went out and then the lawyers. Then they came back and my barrister whispered to me that the judge would be very lenient if I pleaded guilty—a three years conditional discharge. I was pretty down—fed up with it by that time, so I changed to guilty to get it over with.

Case 133 [offer took the form of charge reduction]: On the second day of the trial, the prosecution approached the defence and said that they hadn't got a water-tight case and were prepared to do a deal. They agreed to drop the wounding with intent if I pleaded guilty to wounding. I don't think the judge was involved in the deal—it was a deal the prosecution did with the defence. There was no bargain made over the sentence. I didn't know what sentence I would get although I guessed from the probation officer's report.

Case 141 [a specific offer coupled with charge reduction]: I was pleading not guilty all the way through—I was so adamant in my own mind that I'd be found not guilty. I didn't decide to plead guilty. It was decided for me from what the barrister said to me. He said, 'This is going to drag on for days because they [the prosecution] won't drop these other offences. If you plead guilty to one, they'll drop the others. If you continue to plead not guilty, you'll only antagonise the judge.' He said he'd go and see the judge, something which I don't readily agree with. He said 'My job is wheeling and dealing' and he went to see the judge and said 'He's told me that we'll knock so many offences off and you'll get done for one.' What could I do? I'd been told that the judge had made his findings even before I went into court. The barrister told me even what the judge was going to do [i.e. impose a fine].

In each of these situations, the defendant seemed involved in a plea bargain in the full sense of the term. Offers of a relatively precise nature were made to the defendant—often on a 'take-it-or-leave-it' basis. Before the fairness of these bargains is discussed, it is worthwhile restating the limitations imposed on the judge's involvement in pre-trial plea discussions. The judge, it will be recalled, may discuss a case with counsel, but he must never indicate the *quantum* of sentence he has in mind, only its *form* and then only when he is in a position to say that the sentence will or will not take a particular form whatever plea the accused enters. The rationale behind this appears to be that to allow the judge to participate in any other way would, because of the position he holds in the court system, amount to coercion and render a resulting guilty plea involuntary.

31

In the light of this, an examination of the sub-sample of 22 bargain cases reveals that 13 of the bargains seemed to have been struck within the rules outlined above. Even where the rules have been adhered to, however, there are difficulties. In most of such cases the defendant is given incomplete information: he is told by his barrister what form of sentence he will receive following a guilty plea, without always at the same time being informed that he will receive the same form of sentence if convicted at trial. In these circumstances the influence that this knowledge will have upon the defendant's plea decision is likely to be greater than that where he has received the full information. On a more fundamental level, it is questionable, in our view, whether any of the bargains described by these defendants presented them with a reasonable choice.[26] The issue of the voluntariness of the plea is thus raised, a point to which we shall return later. It is worth noting, however, that in some of these cases the defendant stated that the bargain had been accepted only after considerable additional pressure had been brought to bear upon him by his barrister.

Whilst the fairness of the practice in these 13 cases is perhaps open to doubt, undue pressures were brought to bear in the remaining nine cases if what the defendant described was accurate. In these cases, the judge appeared to place himself in such a position that he was, in effect, inviting the accused to bargain with him, by holding out to the defendant a precise offer or suggestion in which the actual penalties were closely defined. A good illustration of this is *Case 128*, in which the defendant was charged with attempting to obtain property by deception. Before the trial began, he said that his barrister tried to persuade him to plead guilty. He refused to take this advice and then described what happened after the trial began:

The judge sent for my barrister and the prosecution and said, 'As the case stands at the moment I'll be more inclined to give your defendant a suspended sentence but if he goes on pleading not guilty he will go to prison.' So when the barrister told me this I pleaded guilty. I believe it was because the judge didn't want the trial to go on and me to start saying anything against the police.

If the judge involves himself in this way,[27] all talk of the voluntariness of the defendant's plea is meaningless. So far as the defendant is concerned, the question of guilt or innocence is no longer in issue; having, as he sees it, already been found guilty by the judge, his only remaining interest is in minimising the impact of the sentence and, given the judge's statement of intention on this, he has no alternative but to plead guilty. In these circumstances, not only are the adjudication and the sentencing processes merged, but the defendant's freedom is limited to choosing between one form of sentence and another, more severe, form of sentence. That this may subject the defendant to pressure of an extreme kind is not lost on the defendant himself. This is illustrated by the comments of the defendant in the case last cited:

> Obviously I accepted with open arms what the judge said, but it left a bad feeling. I said to the prison officer [in the dock] after the trial, 'So this is British justice!' I'm satisfied with what the judge said but I feel the system is all wrong. I despised him for making a deal; I had no option but to accept.

Even in *Case 141*, cited above, which appears to fall within the *Turner* rules, the defendant in question felt that his plea was very far from being voluntary. The quote continues:

> The barrister came back from seeing the judge and said, 'Well, the judge says we can argue as long as you like but you'll be found guilty anyway.' So I said, 'Where the hell do I stand here?' He said, 'We don't deal in the truth, we deal in facts.' I said, 'Well, British justice is up the wall.' That really sickened me off completely did that. But what could I do? I think I was more forced into it than anything, personally. I was flogging a dead horse. I mean the judge had made up his mind before I even walked through the door.

We shall discuss in a later chapter the extent to which defendants were satisfied with the standard of justice they received, but it is important to note here that, even when an explicit bargain was offered and the defendant was left to make his own decision whether to accept or reject it, less than half of them could be said to be at all satisfied with the outcome of the case. Some felt that the offer had been insufficiently generous, others felt that they had been unduly pressurised into pleading guilty. Interestingly, those defendants who were rated highly by the police on the scales measuring success in 'professional' criminal activity were much more disgruntled about the outcome than others.[28] There are a very small number, it is true, who seemed able to strike a very favourable bargain, but these are exceptional. The two individuals most pleased with the deal were the only two within this group involved in sexual offences. The understandable reluctance of the prosecution in these cases to call the victims (in one case a young child) to give evidence obviously strengthened the defendant's hand in exacting concessions from the prosecution.

A separate, though closely related, group of defendants, consisting of fewer individuals (16 cases in all) than in the plea bargain category, are those who said that, although no explicit offer had been made to them, they had nonetheless understood that their barrister had been able to strike a bargain of some kind on their behalf. We have characterised these cases as of the 'nod-and-the-wink' type. The defendants in question described how an assurance had been offered by counsel and that they had accepted this in good faith. Again a couple of examples will clarify the sorts of bargains we have in mind here.

> Case 68: Barristers always say things like 'If you plead guilty to this, then I'll ...' and it's all hush-hush. They won't come out with what has gone on behind the scenes. It's all on the grapevine and they only let you hear a little bit.

> Case 75: The barrister said, 'I'll do a deal for you. You won't get more than $2\frac{1}{2}$ years [in prison]. The judge knows what's going on, but we can't tell you. Don't think he has come to court this morning knowing nothing about

your case. We have our ways of doing deals and if you plead guilty now, the judge will be lenient—otherwise you'll get 4 years.' I had no alternative but to plead guilty.

More defendants in this group said that the offer took the form of charge reduction than was found with the explicit plea bargain group: in half the cases, the defendant said that the offer took the form of a charge reduction, and in only five cases was a specific offer relating to sentence held out. Nevertheless, these 'nod-and-a-wink' or tacit bargains do not seem different in kind from those in the explicit plea bargain cases. It is true that, in the tacit bargain cases, the barrister is not telling the defendant precisely what is in the judge's mind as to sentence; he may, objectively speaking, be merely *predicting* what form or quantum the sentence will take. But this fine discrimination is of little concern to the defendant. Once the barrister hints that the judge is privy to the deal, the defendant assumes quite naturally that the barrister is merely echoing the thoughts of the judge. When that situation arises, the decision as to plea is made, not upon the advice of the barrister, but upon the assumed intentions of the judge and *Turner* makes clear that in these circumstances it is 'really idle' to think that the defendant had a free choice in the matter of plea.

Although it may be true to say that there is a lower incidence of plea bargaining in England than in the United States, it is not correct to say that bargaining does not exist in England to any significant degree. We found evidence in 22 cases of an explicit bargain being struck and in a further 16 cases of a bargain of a tacit nature. It is disturbing to find that few of the bargains could have left the defendant, in our view, with a genuinely free choice of plea. Most of the offers described by defendants were of such a nature that undue pressure was brought to bear. The assumed limitations on plea bargaining in England count for less in practice than one might suppose, and it is the involvement, real or assumed, of the judge that causes this. Of course the prosecution must be a party to these bargains, but the prosecution's offer of, or consent to, a bargain would be redundant without the involvement of the judge: there can be a bargain only where adherence to its terms can be guaranteed, and in England that necessitates judicial involvement in the deal. Our study suggests that, at least as the defendant understands it from his barrister, there are in Birmingham a very small number of judges (all of circuit judge status or lower) who are not unwilling to involve themselves in such bargains. The fact that defendants claimed to have been offered a specific sentence in return for pleading guilty and that this offer was adhered to in almost every case supports the inference that the judge was involved in the bargain in these cases.[29] As we shall argue in the next chapter, we ourselves are not convinced that the *Turner* rules afford sufficient protection to the defendant from unfair pressures with respect to plea, and many of the bargains described to us by this group of defendants raise, in our view, fundamental questions about the voluntariness of plea.

NOTES AND REFERENCES

1. See, Newman (1956); Newman and NeMoyer (1970); Klein (1972); Smith and Dale (1973). For a rather elaborate exposition, see Ferguson and Roberts (1974).
2. See, for instance, President's Commission *Task Force Report, The Courts* (1967); Chambliss and Seidman (1971) p. 399; Parker (1972); Gallagher (1974).
3. The vast majority of those who claimed to have bargained had previous criminal convictions.
4. Vetri's survey (1964) showed that 86 per cent of the prosecutors responding to a questionnaire he sent out made it a practice to negotiate a guilty plea in appropriate circumstances, and 43 per cent of the respondents said that over half of all guilty pleas were bargained. Other studies have disclosed a higher percentage of bargained pleas: Ariano and Countryman (1969); Blumberg (1967); McIntyre and Lippman (1970); Kress (1974).
5. See particularly, Davis (1971); Jackson (1972); McCabe and Purves (1972a); Klein (1972); Cooper (1972); Heberling (1973).
6. Particularly P. Thomas (1969) and Davis (1971).

7. See D. Thomas (1968); Boulton (1975) p. 75.
8. A lucid discussion of this is given in Davis (1971).
9. For a similar statement, see Alschuler (1968).
10. Devlin (1960) p. 25.
11. Rule 11. See also *A.B.A. Standards for Criminal Justice, Pleas of Guilty* (1968); *U.S.* v. *Rushing*, 456 F.2d 1294 (5th Cir. 1972); *U.S.* v. *Birmingham*, 454 F.2d 706 (10th Cir. 1971).
12. The contention that the fourteenth amendment required state courts to follow Rule 11 was rejected in *Waddy* v. *Heer*, 383 F.2d 789 (6th Cir. 1967). Some states do, however, have a similar requirement to the factual basis rule, for example, Illinois: *People* v. *Morris*, 289 N.E. 2d 635 (1972). See also, *The Trial Judge's Satisfaction as to the Factual Basis of Guilty Pleas*, 1966 Wash.U.L.Q. 306.
13. *People* v. *Foster*, 225 N.E. 2d 200 (N.Y. 1967); *People* v. *Castro*, 44 A.D. 2d 808, 356 N.Y.S. 2d 49 (1974). Cf. *People* v. *Williams*, 44 A.D. 2d 216, 354 N.Y.S. 2d 213 (1974).
14. (1948) 32 Cr.App.R. 136, C.C.A.
15. *Coe* (1969) 53 Cr.App.R. 66, 68.
16. (1970) 54 Cr.App.R. 352.
17. This case also contains important pronouncements on the practice of defence counsel in advising his client on plea. This is discussed further in chapter 3.
18. In *Plimmer* [1975] Crim.L.R. 730, C.A., the court said that, while not wishing to depart from *Turner*, the practice of counsel going to see the judge was in general undesirable.
19. In *Cain* [1976] Crim.L.R. 464, the Court of Appeal said that it was not improper for a judge to inform the accused that a plea of guilty would generally attract a somewhat lighter sentence than a finding of guilt after a contested trial. Such advice should, however, be in general terms. But the court subsequently issued a Practice Direction the substance of which leaves the status of *Cain* in doubt. See Seifman (1976); also *Quartey* [1975] Crim.L.R. 592.
20. According to the case of *Cain* (*op. cit.*), this last 'rule' admits of exceptions, as where counsel, not knowing the judge and being unfamiliar with the tariff, sought guidance from the judge as to the sentence he had in mind so as to enable him properly to advise his client. The rule is that, if the judge gives counsel such information in a precise way, this must not be transmitted to the accused. This might on occasions place counsel in an untenable position: see Seifman (1976).
21. In the United States, most commentators have recognised the desirability of confining the judge's participation in plea bargaining to well-defined situations. The National Advisory Commission on Criminal Justice Standards and Goals has concluded that the court 'should not participate in plea negotiations' (Standard 3.7) and the Federal Rules of Criminal Procedure, Rule 11(e)(1) states that the judge should not participate in plea 'discussions'. See, *Georgia Law Review* (1971); Gallagher (1974).
22. See for instance Bottoms and McClean (1976), especially chapter 1.
23. Bottoms and McClean refer to the practice in Sheffield of 'bail

bargaining' (pp. 200–4), the procedure adopted by the police to with-hold bail until a defendant co-operates. This practice is of little signi-ficance as far as the Birmingham defendants were concerned since all of them, given the nature of the sample, had effectively resisted all pressures and inducements exerted by police and others at earlier stages in the criminal process. See also Heberling (1973) on 'bail bargaining'.

24. We discuss in chapter 5 the extent to which experienced or 'profes-sional' criminals are able to exercise their greater expertise and knowledge to secure favourable bargains.

25. Inevitably this classification of cases is rather crude, both because it is dependent on the extent to which defendants are made aware of what is going on and because the categories themselves are not mutually exclusive.

26. Understandably opinions differ on this. For example, the defence solicitor in *Case 29* stated: 'The judge met counsel privately after the trial had started. As soon as defence cousel informed the defendant that the judge was not intending to send him to prison if convicted of wounding, my client changed his plea to guilty. He was as pleased as punch with the final outcome.' The defendant, however, did not see the bargain in quite this way. He said: 'My barrister told me to plead guilty to one charge. The judge talked to the barrister and solicitor and they begged me to plead guilty. The two of them said the judge had guaranteed that I'd walk out of court [i.e. receive a non-custodial sentence] so eventually I pleaded guilty to please my solicitor, not to please myself.'

27. The defence solicitor concerned in this case provides some independent confirmation of the defendant's story: 'The judge indicated to counsel for the defence in chambers that he would not imprison the defen-dant in the event of a guilty plea. This is what caused the defendant to plead guilty.'

28. This is discussed more fully in chapter 5.

29. Confirmation for this conclusion is provided by several solicitors who returned questionnaires in relation to our study of contested trials. In addition, our informal discussions with local solicitors, barristers and some members of the judiciary have broadly supported this view.

3 PRESSURES BY DEFENCE COUNSEL TO INDUCE A GUILTY PLEA

Between the time of his arrest and his final appearance in court, the defendant will almost invariably be offered advice at some stage to plead guilty. Such advice may come from any one of a number of people: the police, his defence solicitor, members of his family, even his friends, and, where there has been a remand in custody, fellow prisoners and sometimes prison officers. This kind of advice offered to the defendant to plead guilty, from whatever source it came, had in effect been resisted by the defendants in our sample. When they came for trial to the Crown Court, most intended to plead not guilty and the decision to plead guilty was generally a sudden one taken minutes before the time fixed for the court hearing. It is clear from our interviews that the biggest single reason given by defendants for this *volte face* is the advice given by defence counsel.

The influence of defence counsel on the defendant's decision to plead guilty is already apparent from the cases discussed in chapter 2. Those cases primarily involved bargains that counsel appeared to have been able to strike on the defendant's behalf. In this chapter we shall discuss another category in which no bargain was struck but where the defendant stated that the plea of guilty was entered only after pressure of some kind had been brought to bear upon him by his own barrister. As indicated in chapter 2, there are no fewer than 48 defendants who gave as their reason for changing plea advice they had received from counsel. In this discussion we shall be concerned to examine whether the requirement that the defendant shall have a free choice in the matter of plea is met.

It is a basic requirement in English law that a plea of guilty be made freely and, although there has not been the same preoccupation in England as in the United States with the voluntariness of the plea, English courts have from time to time laid down rules that seek to ensure that the defendant's plea has been voluntarily made. One safeguard is that the defendant must himself plead; it is not sufficient for his counsel to plead on his behalf or to indicate that the defendant wishes to plead guilty.[1] In *Ellis* it was said that:

> ... great mischief could ensue if a legal representative was generally regarded as entitled to plead on an accused's behalf. It would open the door to dispute as to whether, for example, counsel had correctly understood and acted upon the instructions which the accused had given him, and, if a dispute of that kind arose, the consequential embarrassment and difficulty could be difficult in the extreme.[2]

Special care is to be taken in the case of an unrepresented defendant to ensure that he understands the elements of the offence to which he is pleading guilty, especially where there is a possible defence disclosed in the depositions.[3] Moreover, a defendant is not to be taken to have admitted that he has committed an offence unless he pleads guilty in plain, unambiguous and unmistakable terms.[4] Not only must the defendant himself plead in plain terms, he must in addition have a free choice of plea. The leading case is again *Turner*.[5] That case, which has already been discussed in chapter 2 in relation to the limits it sets on judicial involvement in plea bargaining, contains important observations also on the role of counsel in the determination of plea: specifically that counsel must be completely free to offer the defendant the best advice he can, if need be in strong terms; that this will often include the advice that a plea of guilty, showing an element of remorse, is a mitigating factor which may well produce a lesser sentence than would otherwise be the case; that counsel will emphasise that the accused must not plead guilty unless he has committed the acts constituting the offence charged; and finally that the defendant himself must have complete freedom of choice as to his plea.[6]

Despite these observations in *Turner*, the present law as to the voluntariness of the plea is far from clear.[7] The sentencing differential between guilty pleas and convictions following not guilty pleas is intended to put some pressure upon defendants to plead guilty, but it is not clear what other pressures may properly be brought to bear. Defence counsel is permitted to put at least some pressure on the defendant to plead guilty, and he may use strong language in doing so, but it will be only in exceptional cases that such pressure will be held to have deprived the accused of a free choice as to plea. How much pressure counsel may properly apply, and what 'strong terms' he may use, has not, however, been made explicit.[8] Our sub-sample of 48 cases, in which the defendants stated that they had entered a plea of guilty only after some pressure had been exerted by counsel, sheds some light upon current practices in this respect.

Our findings disclose evidence of questionable conduct on the part of a small number of barristers in advising defendants on plea. It is by no means easy, of course, for us to draw a rigid distinction between proper and improper advice. What the defendant sees as unreasonable pressure may nonetheless be within the *Turner* rules; alternatively, advice outside the *Turner* rules may be accepted uncomplainingly by him. A more important consideration, to the defendant at least, is not so much whether his barrister strictly adhered to the *Turner* rules in his case, but whether his conduct seemed oppressive or in other ways unreasonable. It is important to make clear that most of the barristers who dealt with cases within this sample were not criticised by their clients; indeed, very many were described to us as men of the highest integrity and wisdom. Only about one in three barristers were criticised, though these tended to be the barristers who dealt with a relatively large number of cases. The following table indicates the extent to which those barristers about whom defendants complained are over-represented in the sample of cases:

	No. of barristers	%	No. of cases dealt with	%
No real complaint made by defendants	43	68.3	70	57.9
Serious criticisms made by defendants	20	31.7	51	42.1

It must be borne in mind throughout the ensuing discussion that, though we draw attention in this chapter and elsewhere to the many serious complaints raised by defendants of their barristers, these complaints relate to less than a third of barristers involved in cases within the sample, as the above table indicates. This minority, however, dealt with a disproportionately large number of cases.[9] Eight barristers, for example, dealt with over one third (46) of the 121 cases in the sample. The views expressed about these eight barristers by the defendants, all of whom were of course interviewed quite independently of each other, are very revealing. Five of the eight barristers received virtually no criticism and, interestingly, remarkably uniform descriptions were given by defendants of them as basically painstaking and sympathetic. The remaining three barristers (who dealt with no fewer than 25 cases) were, on the other hand, seen very commonly as hurried, dismissive or in other ways unsatisfactory. The consistency of the criticisms of these three barristers, together with the virtual absence of criticism of the other five, by defendants who were after all involved in totally independent cases, provides further evidence that the criticisms made by defendants were not without foundation.

It is important to note that we have confined our criticisms to those cases in which serious questions are raised about the voluntariness of plea. Before examining this group of cases, we should state that in a substantial number of cases (20 in the sub-sample) defence counsel unquestionably acted well within the confines of his professional code of ethics and advised the accused as to the propriety and effect of the different courses open to him. Commonly defendants in these cases said that counsel had indicated the weight of evidence against them and the risks they would run in contesting the issue where there was no effective defence to the charge. Counsel had usually pointed out also the possible mitigating effect on sentence that a plea of guilty would produce. Furthermore, it appears from the interviews we have conducted that it was made clear to the defendant that the final decision on plea was his alone and that he should not plead guilty to a charge of which he was innocent. A good illustration is *Case 71* where the defendant, indicted for theft and handling, had his plea of guilty to handling accepted and was sentenced to nine months' imprisonment. He said he had hoped to produce at the trial witnesses who would say that he had bought the property in question in good faith not realising that it was stolen. However, he failed to get the witnesses to come to court and without them he had no real defence. Shortly before the hearing he met his barrister and describes what then took place:

> The barrister raised the question of pleading guilty but he said, 'It's entirely up to you whether you plead guilty or not.' We talked about it for 10 or 15 minutes. But it was my decision—he didn't persuade me, he left it entirely in my hands. He said, 'If you want to plead guilty to the handling charge, we can get the other charge thrown out.' He didn't want to influence me—he advised me all the way along not to plead guilty.

Counsel discussed the possible sentence in these terms:

> He said it is a serious case—but if we can get it down to what you thought it was worth, and, if we can make the judge appreciate that, we might just get a fine or a suspended sentence ... He said that, if I was found guilty after pleading not guilty, I could get some time. He didn't say how long I would get; he said it was entirely up to the judge.

Naturally, the defendant felt that his final decision to plead guilty was influenced more than anything else by the advice that he might get a fine or other non-custodial sentence, but, even after he had been sentenced to a term of imprisonment, he thought that the advice he was given was both realistic and fair and was put in such a way as to leave him the final

43

decision on plea. Similarly in *Case 40*, the defendant was charged with obtaining a car by deception and handling it. Eventually, he pleaded guilty to the handling charge:

> I took the advice of my barrister. It was a lesser charge and my barrister said, 'I'm not going to advise you to plead guilty to something you didn't do, but the way it looks you are going to be found guilty and you will get a bigger sentence for wasting the court's time.' It was my decision to plead guilty and the mitigation the barrister put forward was handled well.

As is to be expected, the advice of the barrister may be based upon one or more of a number of factors that any counsel must properly consider relevant. It may be, for example, that the defendant in talking to his barrister has shown himself to be untrustworthy or unreliable and, in such circumstances, the barrister might well feel it necessary to indicate to the defendant that it would be hazardous to contest the case and expose himself to cross-examination. Again, counsel may be aware of the sentencing propensities of a particular judge before whom the defendant is to appear, and, if this is the case, the defendant may well be heavily influenced by this information. One defendant, *Case 150*, charged with burglary, reported his conversation with counsel in the following way:

> When I got to court my barrister said I stood no chance pleading not guilty. He said that I might as well plead guilty and get it dealt with. I wasn't sure but then he said, 'I've looked through your case and I would plead guilty. It would stand better if you plead guilty because this judge gives Green Shield Stamps for pleading guilty' and he laughed. I said, 'Yes, all right' and he said, 'You stand no chance really; you'd be found guilty anyway.'

One clear characteristic of this sub-group of 20 cases is that counsel is very careful in advising on the possible sentence: no false expectations are held out and usually the advice is in general terms. Thus, in *Case 143*, the defendant describes how he finally decided to plead guilty to handling:

> Up to the stage when I went up for plea, I was all for

44

pleading not guilty. The barrister said on the day that I had a slim chance if I pleaded not guilty; he said I hadn't got a defence. He said, 'The best thing you can do is plead guilty. If you plead guilty, I'll do my best for you. You've got a fair judge and I'll put the case over to him, explain you knew nothing about [the theft] and that by pleading guilty you will save the court's time.' And that's what he did.

There are indications in some of the cases within this group that counsel may have transgressed the *Turner* rules or placed unreasonable pressure on a defendant, but these indications were not sufficiently clear-cut to cause us to doubt the propriety of counsel's behaviour in advising the defendant. However, in the remaining 28 cases in this sub-sample, there was evidence that the advice counsel gave was of such a nature that no reasonable person could say that it was fair or proper or that the final decision to plead guilty was made voluntarily. As we shall make clear in due course, no criticism of members of the Bar is necessarily intended here. Indeed, as we argue in the concluding chapter, the judicial system itself (and particularly the discount in sentence which usually follows upon a guilty plea) imposes severe restrictions and pressures on those whose duty it is to advise the defendant on plea. Though on occasions the advice given to defendants may, in a strict sense, contravene established ethical standards, it may nonetheless (whatever the defendant or anyone else may think) be in the best interests of the client.

In this group of 28 cases, most of the defendants felt, by the manner in which the advice was given, that they were being encouraged to take no active part in the determination of plea. The courts have sanctioned the practice of counsel giving advice 'if need be in strong terms' to the defendant, but they have not made any more explicit what is meant by 'strong terms' and there is no indication that the court appreciates that some defendants may be weaker and more compliant than others. Occasionally the advice given is in very strong terms but counsel indicates that the defendant may still plead not guilty if he wishes. This sometimes leaves the defendant with the distinct impression that he has no effective choice in the matter; as the defendant in *Case 44* put it:

> The barrister didn't actually force me to plead guilty, but the way he put it I'd have to be some kind of nut if I didn't plead guilty.

But no fewer than 23 of the 28 defendants in this group of cases said that they were given no alternative but to plead guilty and that their barrister had 'instructed' or 'ordered' or 'forced' or even, on one occasion, 'terrorised' them into pleading guilty. Now it may well be the case that this is not what happened in reality in these instances, but the important point is that this is how the defendants in question *perceived* the advice of their barrister. This is what they believed had happened. This perception of the nature of the relationship with the barrister is all the more disturbing because it was said in *Turner* that only in extreme cases will the defendant be able to argue that counsel's advice was such as to deprive him of a free choice over plea. It is the case that the defendant's solicitor, or his representative, is invariably present when the defendant meets his barrister and his presence ought to represent a restraining influence on any barrister attempting to exert undue pressure on a reluctant defendant. What has been happening, however, in recent years is that this check has been eroded as solicitors have increasingly sent to court for this purpose junior assistants, who are unequal to the task of upholding a defendant's rights were this necessary.[10]

Any discussion with the defendant about the possible courses of action open to him normally includes some talk about sentencing, a factor usually uppermost in the defendant's mind. No other single consideration acts as such a powerful inducement to plead guilty as the fact that he may expect a more lenient sentence if he pleads guilty than if he contests the matter. It appears that counsel on occasions regard as significant matters that are not usually thought to be relevant sentencing considerations. Although a guilty plea, showing an element of remorse, may be a mitigating factor

46

in sentencing, the authorities clearly establish that the conduct of the defence at trial does not justify any increase in sentence above what is appropriate for the offence. Thus, in *Thomas and Whittle*[11] the court said:

> It is no doubt deplorable to make an unjustifiable attack on the honesty of any witness but it is not a criminal offence in itself and it is not a matter that can be taken into consideration so as to add anything to the sentence ... [T]he appropriate sentence cannot be increased by an attack that may be made on the credibility of any witness.

This, however, is not a view apparently shared by some barristers. Many defendants in the sample said that they were told that their proposed defence (particularly where an attack upon police witnesses was contemplated) could not be run without risking incurring the wrath of the trial judge and a consequent substantial increase in sentence. Those with prior criminal records in particular were singled out as being vulnerable in these circumstances. The defendant in *Case 100*, charged with wounding, discussed his plea with counsel in these terms:

> My barrister kept saying I had no chance and that it would be bad if I fought it in court. He said, 'Well what I'll do, if you plead guilty...' and I said, 'No way, I'm not having it; this copper has made up verbals.' The barrister said, 'If you stick to your plea of not guilty, it seems to me there is going to be some right mud-slinging towards the police. If you do get found guilty, as you will on something, the judge is going to say, "You don't like the police—our blokes—and all these allegations were made to try and cover yourself up for striking this poor [victim]," and you'll get done very heavily.'

Again, in *Case 114*:

> My barrister came to see me just before the trial and said, 'Hello, what are you doing?' When I said I was pleading not guilty, he said, 'Oh' and he threw a fit—I could see it in his face. Maybe he wanted to get home early but he just didn't want to know. He hadn't even bothered to look at the papers. He was useless. He said, 'Plead guilty definitely. All this mud that you want to sling at the prosecution and the police, it's all going to come back on you.'

47

It might be the case that, despite the accepted sentencing standards, counsel is right in his view that a particular sort of defence will attract an increased sentence. Indeed, as we discuss in chapter 4, the fact that counsel may advise defendants not to run a particular defence, especially where this involves an attack upon police evidence, will often be realistic and sound in the sense that to run such a defence might well have an adverse effect upon sentence. Moreover, even highly skilled advocates would find it extremely difficult to establish (if it were the truth) that a police witness was lying. If that be right, it is certainly arguable that any competent legal adviser would be failing in his duty if he did not forcibly point out to the defendant the grave risks that are likely to follow if he requires the defence to be conducted on the basis that the police are liars. In either event, however, it discloses a disturbing situation. For if some judges do regard the defence run as justifying an aggravation of sentence, not only are they contravening established sentencing criteria, but it is also the case that the defendant is unable to challenge the sentence on that basis in those cases where the judge has not made this fact explicit.[12] If, on the other hand, counsel are wrong in their view that judges do have regard to such factors, then it seems that many defendants are being given misleading advice and are being induced to plead guilty upon a false basis. In any event, we would argue that it is more appropriate that the whole question be brought into the open and that barristers should not be required to decide critical questions of this nature.

Related to this is the more general question of the discount to be given following a guilty plea. The Court of Appeal, in *Cain*,[13] is reported recently to have said:

> ... it was trite to say that a plea of guilty would generally attract a somewhat lighter sentence than a plea of not guilty after a full dress-contest on the issue. Everybody knew that it was so, and there was no doubt about it. Any accused person who did not know about it should know it. The sooner he knew the better.

An accused person may, or must, now be told that a guilty

plea may be a mitigating factor, but a judge is permitted to indicate this fact only in general terms; any precise offer or suggestion on the part of the judge is to be condemned.[14] Similarly, counsel is not permitted to inform the accused of the precise penalties the judge has in mind, except in the sense covered in *Turner*. There would, however, appear to be no constraints upon counsel expressing his own view as to the likely sentence, and our cases provide evidence that counsel considers it a proper part of his duty to discuss sentencing differentials with the accused. Many pleas of course follow from the defendant's expectation that an indefinite, but substantial, degree of leniency will follow a guilty plea. This is common where counsel has refused to be drawn on the question of the likely sentence or has indicated only in a vague way that it may be lower on a plea of guilty, and in those cases where defendants are themselves aware that judges normally sentence more leniently in such circumstances. In ten cases, however, the most decisive factor influencing a defendant's decision to plead guilty was said to be the way in which the sentencing alternatives were put to him by counsel. In *Case 134* the defendant faced several counts of trafficking in drugs and one count of assaulting his girlfriend. The defendant did not dispute that he had received money from dealings in drugs, but he wanted to contest strongly the gravity of the allegations, the sums of money involved, and he totally denied the charge of assault. After discussing the matter with his barrister, he entered pleas of guilty to all charges in the course of the prosecution's evidence, and received three years' imprisonment:

> I was really forced to plead guilty. I was feeling pleased because the witnesses didn't say much about me in their evidence; only two of them did and one of these said, 'It was just a few pounds.' But then my barrister and solicitor took me down below and they said, 'Look, you've got no chance, so you will plead guilty.' I said, 'I don't want to plead guilty, they are very bad charges against me and I didn't assault her and it was only a few quid.' The barrister then said, 'If you're found guilty you will get about 10 or 15 years but if you plead guilty you will get 4 or 5 years.'

I was really shocked. I was so scared, sweating and nervous and he frightened me with this 10–15 years stuff and saying I had no chance. They then talked to my mother and frightened her as well. They brought her down to see me and they persuaded her and she said, 'If they think you are going to get 10–15 years if you plead not guilty, you might as well plead guilty.' I agreed to plead guilty but it wasn't my decision; I had no choice about it. I was very frightened by everything. It was a split second decision; I had to make a decision then and there, when I was very nervous and being scared by 10–15 years.

The defendant in *Case 60* faced a similar predicament. Charged with various offences he eventually had his plea of guilty to the least serious count accepted and was given a suspended sentence. He described his discussion with counsel in these terms:

My barrister compelled me to plead guilty. He threatened me saying, 'You will go to gaol for three years if you plead not guilty, the case will go on for a long time and you will have to pay all the expenses which will come to £400. But if you plead guilty you will just get a fine.' He wouldn't listen to what I had to say; he compelled me to plead guilty.

These cases, and there are ten altogether of a similar kind, hardly require comment. The *quantum* of the discount that will normally be given for a plea of guilty is not known but our own informal discussions with various judges suggest that something between one quarter and one third of the sentence is likely to be discounted for a plea of guilty. Whether this is so or not, however, there must come a point when the alternatives presented to the defendant are such as to amount to undue pressure in the sense that the defendant dare not take the risk of contesting the case. In the face of advice such as that described in the two examples above, it cannot be seriously argued that a defendant has a free choice of plea; in such cases his choice is clear but the disparity between the sentences is so unconscionable that he is in effect deprived of the capacity to make a reasoned decision. In such cases, an accused is being confronted with an unreasonable choice that

50

may even sometimes cause a man to plead guilty to a charge of which he protests his innocence.[15]

In three cases, defendants said that they were deprived of a free choice of plea by subterfuge and tricks.[16] The defendant in *Case 73* was charged with theft of property from a school and taking a conveyance without authority. He said that he had told both his solicitor and barrister that he had committed the theft but he disputed the amount of property taken and he claimed to be totally innocent of the second charge. After seeing his barrister, he pleaded guilty to both charges and was sentenced to eighteen months' imprisonment. After recounting the disputed matters on the theft charge, the defendant continued:

> Also there was a stolen car and it was my mate who took it, but the police charged me with it and I can't even drive. I told my barrister this and he said, 'Well, just plead guilty to this, it will just be taken into consideration, and I will recommend probation.' But when I went up into court I was charged with it [taking the car], and the barrister said, 'There's nothing to worry about, just plead guilty to it.' He told me he would recommend probation, but he changed it in court and recommended a short prison sentence. I think it's bad really. He sort of pulled a fast one on me. I think he just wanted to get it over with.

An even more disturbing case concerned joint defendants, Mick (*Case 86*) and Terry (*Case 87*), who were charged with possessing cannabis and assaulting the police. When arrested they both claimed that Mick was assaulted with a truncheon by the police and that they then both struck the police officers involved. None of the matters recounted by the defendants, who were interviewed separately in prison, was ventilated in open court when both pleaded guilty. Nor had they the opportunity after the trial to invent a common story. Nevertheless, the stories they told tallied in every material respect. Each had decided before the court hearing that they would contest the assault charge. Each was separately represented. It is worth citing each defendant's story at some length. On the morning of the hearing, Terry's barrister came

51

to see him and advised him to plead guilty to possessing cannabis and to assaulting the police, but he initially refused:

> So I said, 'No, I want it that way. I am pleading guilty to possession, and they [the police] have turned the story inside out—we were assaulted by the police.' I said, 'You can look at the photographs of us taken after the arrest.' At that point one of the screws [lock-up officers] came down and said to the barrister, 'Your clerk is here.' The barrister says, 'Excuse me' and went away, and he is only away for the space of two minutes. He got back and said, 'Things have changed; [Mick] will plead guilty to possessing cannabis and guilty to the assault.' I said, 'Is there anything to get Mick down here as I don't think you've got it right; he's pleading not guilty.' So he says, 'We can't bring Mick down here because of the circumstances of the offence.' So I said, 'It's silly, he's given himself a year.' He says, 'Well, he's doing that.' So I thought to myself, when we get into court and we stand in the dock, I'll ask Mick, 'Did you say that?' So when we got into the dock I says to Mick, 'What did you plead guilty for?' He says, 'Well I had to because of your plea.' His words were that his barrister told him that I was pleading guilty. I said, 'No, that's not right; I told him I would plead guilty only to possession.'

Mick's version of the events is as follows:

> The barrister made me change my mind and plead guilty to the two charges. He tricked me, he bamboozled me. He didn't say I had to plead guilty, but he told me that Terry was going to plead guilty to assault. This left me with no choice. I told him I was pleading not guilty and he went out like, the barrister, and he came back and says, 'Well, Terry will plead guilty to the assault and to the possession.' So I had to do the same. But the barrister had said the same to my mate Terry that I'd agreed to plead guilty, which I hadn't. I didn't get a chance to speak to Terry until we were in the dock and when I found out what had happened, well, by then it was too late. The sentence was fair, quite reasonable. I was pissed off about the barrister though; he bamboozled me, he tricked me into pleading guilty.

These three cases (73, 86, 87), and there are others of a less extreme nature within the sample, raise doubts as to whether the barristers in question were acting in a manner befitting their true professional position. The credence to be attached to these stories is greatly strengthened by the fact that all three defendants were well satisfied with the way their solicitors had handled their cases prior to the day of trial, and that none of them felt aggrieved at the sentences they received. That each of the defendants was satisfied that a rough sort of justice had been done cannot, however, minimise concern over the way they had decided upon a plea of guilty. A barrister may advise his client to plead guilty, but it is not proper for him to usurp the function of the court when the issue is to be contested and compel a guilty plea; to do so is to embark upon a course contrary to accepted principles of criminal justice. If such barristers take upon themselves the function of deciding upon the guilt or innocence of defendants, the adversarial system of justice itself is threatened. This is particularly so in those cases where the accused asserts his innocence. We shall return to this subject in the next chapter, but it is important, in this context, to recall the duty of counsel in such circumstances. This was made clear in *Turner*, where the Court of Appeal observed:

> Counsel, of course, will emphasize that the accused must not plead guilty unless he has committed the acts constituting the offence charged.

It appears, however, that in a disturbingly large number of cases even a strong assertion of innocence may be treated with indifference by certain barristers. The observation in *Turner* has little correspondence with reality in these cases: it appears to us to be the case that, when certain barristers decide that the accused ought to plead guilty, they are prepared to go even to extreme lengths to bend the will of a reluctant client. One example will suffice here, and we shall deal more systematically with this question later:

> *Case 136*: My barrister pleaded guilty for me. I told him that I was innocent but he said I was a bloody nuisance and that nobody would believe me. He said, 'The judge and the others will never believe what you say in court; they will always believe the police.' I said, 'How can this

53

be so? What I am saying is true.' He said I must plead guilty—I even argued with him in court. This was wrong; the barrister decided my plea for me. I always remember in my mind saying, 'You should not plead guilty for me.' I was forced to plead guilty by my barrister; it was wrong of him.

The picture presented by many of the examples cited here is clearly at variance with the accepted view of the plea determination process in England. Although the courts accept that limited pressures may be exerted on an accused person to induce him to plead guilty, and have not articulated in detail the safeguards that should attend the pre-court consultations, it cannot possibly be imagined that they would condone the sorts of practices many defendants described to us. In a system where plea negotiation is very often conducted in secret, the defendant's reliance upon his own barrister is almost total. If a barrister transgresses rules laid down by the courts or fails to conform to accepted ethical standards of behaviour, the accused is left very largely without redress.[17] Some complaints of defendants may be attributable to misunderstandings, but misunderstandings are an in-built feature of an unregulated and covert system. In other circumstances, the defendant's plea is often conditioned by his expectation of what will happen to him at trial or on sentence and this expectation is one he principally gets from defence counsel. It is all the more important, therefore, that counsel's advice be careful and reasoned; it should never be put in such a way that the defendant perceives it as an order, and it is insupportable that it should subjugate the will or destroy the volition of the defendant.

One reason for this unsatisfactory state of affairs is the hasty manner in which pre-trial consultations are often conducted.[18] Except where the defendant has early on expressed an intention to plead not guilty for purely tactical reasons, the final decision to plead guilty is often a sudden one, taken in circumstances likely to be disadvantageous to the defendant. Mentally prepared for a trial, often with the active encouragement of his solicitor, the defendant suddenly experi-

54

ences before the hearing a hostile and friendless environment. Often his solicitor has been unable or unwilling to attend, an assistant having been sent instead, and the assistant is much less hopeful of the defendant's chances, preferring to leave the barrister to advise the defendant. The defendant is already in a tense and agitated state, unsure of how his case stands, when the barrister appears, frequently only a few minutes before the time set for the court hearing. Now is the time, the defendant imagines, when he will discuss his case with his barrister and instruct him. The barrister, however, makes it clear from the outset that the case is hopeless and that a plea of guilty ought without question to be entered. The defendant is unwilling to do this, but the barrister is not to be deflected: the pressure on the defendant is increased until no further resistance is met. Such, at any rate, is the picture given by very many defendants in our sample, of which the following cases are but two examples:

Case 114 (referred to earlier): There were a million and one things I wanted to say to the barrister if only I could have had the time. There was a lot to say but when the barrister only comes in a few minutes before you go into court there's not a lot you can say, and, anyway, he just didn't want to know.

Case 107: I told the barrister I was not guilty on one of the charges but he told me to plead guilty to it anyway. He was happy when I pleaded guilty, but I wasn't. Barristers couldn't care less about you, he only told me to plead guilty to make his job easier. It was all too rushed. When I pleaded guilty, the barrister looked at me in court and smiled as if to say, 'That's right, you've done the right thing.'

It is not, however, merely a question of allowing the defendant insufficient time to consider his plea. It is also a question of the attitude displayed towards the defendant. Many of our defendants drew attention to the fact that counsel was not familiar with the brief[19] and was not interested in the case unless the defendant was prepared to plead guilty:

Case 15: I only saw my barrister for 3 minutes before I went

55

into court. He didn't even listen to what I had to say—he was rushing off somewhere else so he was in a hurry to get the case over. He just didn't want to know.

Case 60: I don't think the barrister even opened the file and he didn't listen to what I wanted to say; he just compelled me to plead guilty.

Case 73: I was talking to my barrister for about 10 minutes. He didn't know much about my case; he was going on what the probation officer had told him and he didn't even know that. He didn't know much about my case at all.

Although the courts have frequently declared that the defendant must have a free choice in the matter of plea, it appears that this requirement is not always satisfied in practice. As we have seen in chapter 2, a very small number of judges seemingly stray outside the restrictions on their involvement laid down by the courts in such a way that the defendant has no real alternative but to plead guilty. But the person the defendant sees as representing the greatest threat to his freedom of choice is his own barrister. The high ethical standards of the profession are a by-word in legal writings, but they do not seem always to be matched by reality. Advice is not infrequently taken by defendants as an order; protestations of innocence may be ignored or summarily dismissed; sentencing differentials of a grossly inflated nature threatened; and the sentencing propensities of the judge used as a stick to beat the unwilling. Indeed, in our view, the public image of the barrister fearlessly upholding the interests of his client without regard to any unpleasant consequences, either to himself or to any other person, represents in such cases a considerable distortion of the truth.

NOTES AND REFERENCES

1. *R.* v. *Heyes* [1951] 1 K.B. 29, C.C.A.; *R.* v. *Ellis* (1973) 57 Cr.App.R. 571, C.A. Cf. *R.* v. *Ali Tasamulug* [1971] Crim.L.R. 441.
2. *Ibid.*, pp. 574–5.
3. *R.* v. *Griffiths* (1932) 23 Cr.App.R. 153, C.C.A.

4. *R.* v. *Golathan* (1915) 84 L.J.K.B. 758, C.C.A. And see *R.* v. *Baker* (1912) 28 T.L.R. 363, C.C.A.; *R.* v. *Alexander* (1912) 7 Cr.App.R. 110; *R.* v. *Ingleson* [1915] 1 K.B. 512, C.C.A.; *R.* v. *Lloyd* (1923) 17 Cr. App.R. 184.

5. (1970) 54 Cr.App.R. 352.

6. And see *R.* v. *Hall* (1968) 52 Cr.App.R. 528, p. 534.

7. In *R.* v. *Plimmer* [1975] Crim.L.R. 730, the Court said that, while not wishing to depart from *Turner*, the practice of counsel going to see judges was in general undesirable.

8. The latest edition (6th) of *Conduct and Etiquette at the Bar* by Sir William Boulton confines itself to the *Turner* observations: see pp. 72–3.

9. Certain barristers were considerably over-represented within this group of late changes of plea in that they did not appear to anything like the same extent within our separate sample of 500 contested trials, or even amongst a group of 2,000 guilty plea cases heard in the Birmingham Crown Court within the same time period. It is very interesting also to note that some of the barristers who dealt with a large number of the 500 contested trials were not involved at all in this separate sample of late changes of plea. Why these different patterns of involvement on the part of barristers are found must remain a matter of conjecture. (See also on this, Bottoms and McClean, 1976, p. 130.)

10. Many members of the legal profession have in the course of our research complained to us that levels of the present attendance fees paid to solicitors for this purpose are inadequate.

11. Unreported, cited in D. A. Thomas (1970), pp. 53–4. And see, *Regan* [1959] Crim. L.R. 529; *Kelly* [1961] Crim. L.R. 564; *Claxton* [1965] Crim.L.R. 737; *Dunbar* (1966) 51 Cr.App.R. 57.

12. The judge is not of course obliged to give reasons for the sentence imposed.

13. *Op. cit.* Cf. *O'Leary* [1965] Crim.L.R. 56.

14. *Cain, op. cit.*

15. See, for example, 1966 *Annual Survey of American Law*, pp. 537–52, where the following rule is recommended: 'A defendant cannot be confronted during the bargaining process with alternatives which raise a substantial possibility that they might cause an innocent man to plead guilty. If he is confronted with such alternatives, his plea will not be voluntary, however legitimate the motives of those who offer or agree to the bargain' (p. 545). Cf. *Hall* (1968) 52 Cr.App.R. 528 in which counsel told the defendant that conviction of the greater charge might lead to a sentence of 10–12 years imprisonment, whereas a plea of guilty to a lesser count would probably reduce the sentence to one of 5–7 years.

16. Cf. *Chadwicke, The Times*, 22 November 1932, C.C.A. where the court granted leave to appeal against conviction and sentence in a case in which it was alleged that the defendant was tricked into pleading guilty by a police officer's promise that if he did so he would be bound over.

17. On this point, see Heberling (1973) who notes that, in relation to the question of counsel using undue influence in advising a guilty plea,

'reviewing courts generally disbelieve the defendant's allegations and phrase their judgments in terms of vague statements of professional ethics. Since the case law and judicial control have not developed in this area, the quality of representation the Anglo-American defendant receives is essentially a matter of the ethical standards of his legal adviser' (p. 457).

18. Similar evidence of the somewhat superficial treatment that defendants often receive from counsel is found in Zander's study (1972b) and in Bottoms and McClean (1976, pp. 158–9).

19. We have no way of ascertaining whether defendants were justified in this view. All we can say is that the point was raised spontaneously by so many defendants that it appeared unwise to disregard it.

4 CLAIMING INNOCENCE YET PLEADING GUILTY

In the previous two chapters we have described in some detail the considerable pressures and inducements that some of the defendants in our sample of cases said had been brought to bear on them and the way in which many of them felt they were forced to plead guilty. It is perhaps arguable, though we would not ourselves adopt this position, that none of these instances need give rise to public alarm if, at the end of the day, justice is done; in other words, if the courts succeed in convicting the guilty and acquitting the innocent, it does not matter overmuch if procedural flaws are disclosed. Whatever the merits or otherwise of this position, the evidence from our research suggests that the system of criminal justice that we have examined here distinguishes only crudely between the genuinely guilty and the genuinely innocent. We shall present, in the course of this chapter, findings that indicate that some people who may have been innocent, and a larger group who may well have been acquitted had the case gone to trial, were in fact induced to plead guilty. In this chapter, we shall be concerned to identify those factors that cause such people to plead guilty.

The main aim of the English system of criminal procedure, at least for contested trials, is to ensure the conviction of the guilty without at the same time convicting the innocent. In order to achieve this central aim, the system has developed certain safeguards at trial; these include the heavy burden of proof on the prosecution to prove the case beyond reasonable doubt, the presumption that an accused person is innocent until proved guilty, and the strict rules surrounding the reception of evidence. Whether such safeguards adequately protect against the risk of convicting an innocent man is an open question, but their existence in the trial system raises the question whether any other form of criminal procedure that lacks such safeguards carries with it an increased risk to innocent men. The research evidence to date on this question is inconclusive. This research, which has been carried out both in England and in the United States, strongly suggests that a number of innocent defendants may for a variety of reasons plead guilty at their trial. Blumberg (1967), for example, examined the cases of over 700 defendants who had pleaded guilty in a Metropolitan court in the United States. He found that no fewer than 51 per cent of them claimed to be innocent in some measure, though with varying degrees of fervour and credibility. The commonest reasons for this were basically pragmatic—'you can't beat the system' or else 'I wanted to get it over with'. Contrary to the popular assumption that it is the police or prosecuting counsel who are most influential in persuading defendants to plead guilty, Blumberg noted that in 57 per cent of his cases it was the defendant's own lawyer who was most instrumental in eliciting a guilty plea.

In England, some light has been shed on the question of innocent people pleading guilty by three studies, though the findings are to some extent contradictory. The first of these studies, conducted by Davies (1970), was principally concerned with the operation of the bail system. In the course of interviewing over 400 men charged with burglary and related offences, eight defendants volunteered the information that they intended to plead guilty although they claimed to be innocent of the charges, and a further 21, who earlier had said that they would plead not guilty or otherwise denied guilt, at the end in court pleaded guilty. Similarly Dell's (1971) research, concerned with women prisoners in Holloway, indicated that about one in seven of women in the sample who had pleaded guilty in the Magistrates' Courts and had been sentenced to terms of imprisonment, denied when interviewed subsequently that they had in fact committed the offences in question. The main reasons given in each of these studies for the apparently anomalous decision as to plea are similar: a belief that the defendant's word will be disregarded if it contradicts police evidence; that it is better to co-operate with the police than to oppose them; that a lighter sentence is likely to follow a guilty plea, and the like. One of the most disturbing aspects of Dell's study was the proportion (25 per cent) of what she calls 'inconsistent pleaders' who had no previous convictions, the majority of whom gave police advice or pressure as their reason for pleading guilty. It is perhaps less likely that this fact would be as decisive in influencing a defendant to plead guilty in the Crown Court. Indeed, in the most recent study of this type, confined to cases in which the defendant pleaded guilty at the Crown Court, McCabe and Purves (1972a) concluded that there was no evidence that the police had behaved improperly or oppressively in order to induce the defendant to plead guilty. Nor could they find any evidence indicating that any defendant in their sample of cases was 'substantially innocent'. Their main conclusion was that the guilty plea represented a realistic approach to the situation facing the accused and had not been induced by oppression or made in ignorance or bewilderment.

In Dell's study of women prisoners, no fewer than 80 per cent were without legal representation in court. She sees this fact as critical in understanding the phenomenon of 'inconsistent pleading'[1] and notes that:

Inconsistent pleading, whether in response to police persuasion or other causes, would certainly diminish if it could be ensured that every accused person had the chance of speaking to a legal adviser before the plea is entered. [p. 36]

Despite the fact that in our Birmingham sample this condition is universally met, since all defendants without exception were legally represented, we found that over half of the sample made some claim to be innocent, and often very vehemently, either of the whole of the indictment to which they pleaded guilty or of individual counts within it. It would clearly have been a mistake to have asked defendants outright whether they were innocent or not of the charges to which they pleaded guilty. At the time the interview schedule was devised, we would doubtless have considered this to have been irrelevant to all but a tiny proportion of respondents. But, in any event, to have asked defendants such a question directly might well have provoked a thoroughly artificial reply,[2] defendants feeling that they ought to make at least a token claim to innocence if only to keep up appearances in an interview. So no question was included in the interview schedule relating to guilt or otherwise of respondents and, in the discussion that follows, it must be borne in mind that all claims of innocence were volunteered spontaneously by respondents and were not in any way provoked by our questioning them on the subject. Needless to say, such claims of innocence cannot be accepted at their face value; indeed, the defendant's conception of innocence often does not accord with the legal conception. For example, defendants involved in offences of violence sometimes wrongly claimed to have been innocent because they said they had been provoked by the victim; provocation would, however, not have been a defence in these cases.[3] We attempted to distinguish the types of claims of innocence made by different respondents. The following table sets out the types of distinctions that were made.

Defendants' claims of innocence	No.	%
The defendant makes no claim of innocence in course of interview	51	42.2
The defendant makes only a token protestation of innocence	13	10.7
The defendant makes a strong protestation of innocence in relation to all charges to which he pleaded guilty	33	27.3
The defendant makes a strong protestation of innocence in relation to some of the charges to which he pleaded guilty	12	9.9
The defendant is uncertain whether what he did was in fact criminal	12	9.9
	121	100.0

The table thus discloses the disturbing finding that no less than 70 of the 121 defendants interviewed (57.8 per cent) made some claim to be innocent. It must immediately be stated that many of these claims were, to say the least, somewhat limp; others, it is true, were scarcely believable and seemed far-fetched to the interviewer; still others were, as noted above, based on a misunderstanding of the law. But these considerations should not be allowed to disguise the fact that there were, within this sample of defendants, a number whose stories simply could not be lightly dismissed. Many, indeed, were indignantly protesting that their barrister had done just that. For obvious reasons it cannot ever be ascertained whether these claims of innocence were in reality justified, but it is possible, by using the predictions made by the two independent case assessors, at least to make an estimate of the likelihood of their being acquitted at trial had they resisted the sorts of offers or pressures described in the previous two chapters. In the examination that follows, we shall not discuss the token claims of innocence made by the 13 defendants identified in the table above. In these cases, the defendants' account seemed to the interviewer to be palpably untrue and we shall concentrate on the 57 individuals who made more substantial claims. It is interesting to note in passing that there is no relationship whatever between these claims of innocence and the basic reasons given by defendants for pleading guilty. In other words, there were proportionately as many of these defendants who said they had pleaded guilty because they were tempted by the bargains that had been offered to them as pleaded guilty in response to the other kinds of inducements and pressures described earlier.

We shall argue that the evidence from our study demonstrates that induced or negotiated guilty pleas are an inaccurate method of disposition of cases in the sense that there are several defendants who maintain their innocence and whose cases might well have resulted in an acquittal. We shall present additional evidence of comparable pressures brought to bear upon several defendants who resisted pleading guilty and were ultimately acquitted at trial. Some of these defendants were, in the view of the judge, solicitors and the police involved in the case, rightly acquitted.

Before embarking upon an examination of the claims of innocence, it is worthwhile noting the small group of cases (12) in which the defendant when interviewed expressed uncertainty about whether what he did was in fact criminal. The majority of such cases involved offences of violence in which the defendant did not deny that he had struck the victim a blow. In these cases, the defendant's uncertainty arose out of what he saw as a distorted account of the incident in question being presented unchallenged to the court. The defendant commonly felt that, had an accurate picture of the circumstances surrounding the wounding or assault been given, he would have been acquitted or, at least, given a much less severe sentence. Each defendant said he had been told by his barrister that he would be convicted at trial, that it was dangerous to contest the case and that matters such as self-defence ought not to be put forward. Sometimes this advice was said to have been accompanied by the promise of a relatively lenient sentence and, as one defendant observed, 'in these circumstances I decided it's better to be a free coward than a locked-up hero.' It seems that at no point in the proceedings, whether before or after sentence, was it ever explained to the defendant why, if this were so, matters highly relevant to the charge could not be raised at court. One serious consequence of this is that these defendants not only resented the unjust treatment they felt they had received but bore a deep sense of grievance against a system that appeared so weighted that counsel could only advise them that they could not even risk challenging allegedly untrue or unfair evidence.

The twelve defendants who denied involvement in some of the charges only are an important group. The mere fact that they were prepared to admit to us that they were guilty of some of the offences charged lends credence to their stories. Additionally, most of these defendants recognised that their pleas of guilty to the charge of which they protested innocence did not adversely affect the overall sentence. That is to say, they believed that their sentences would have been the same had they made accurate pleas to the charges in the indictment; their complaints were more concerned with what they saw as the sham nature of the guilty plea procedure than with any adverse consequences suffered as a result of the inaccurate plea. An example of this sort of claim is given by the defendant in *Case 68*. This involved a youth who admitted damaging property but who vehemently denied two related charges of theft:

> I made a mistake the first time I went up to Crown Court because the barrister said to me, 'What I want you to do is plead guilty to attempted theft and criminal damage.' Well I said, 'No, I had no intention of taking anything.' But then I changed my mind. He put the frighteners on me —he said, 'If you plead not guilty, the trial will be put off and you'll have to go down the stairs [i.e. be remanded in custody] until the next trial. But if you plead guilty, we'll try and fit it in this afternoon.' So I'm thinking that if I'm going to have to wait a month or two in custody, I might as well get it over with now. I was going to plead guilty to the damage but I didn't see why I should have to carry the can for the other two charges. I only changed my mind after seeing the barrister. I've straightened it out now—I should never have pleaded guilty to the attempted theft. I regret doing that though I don't really blame the barrister for it. The jury might have found me guilty anyway.

The defendants who strongly protest their innocence with respect to all charges to which they pleaded guilty said they did so on the whole for similar kinds of reasons. The commonest reasons given by defendants were the feeling of hopelessness at attempting to rebut the evidence of police officers and the severity of sentence they anticipated if they failed to do so; the weariness caused by the case dragging on for months on end and the consequent anxiety and social disruption caused by frequent remands (especially if in custody); the attractiveness of a bargain held out to them or perhaps merely the negative pressure exerted by counsel. Having examined a number of such cases, we would contend that *anyone*, and not just those with long criminal records, may

65

face a set of circumstances where the only reasonable alternative open to them is in fact to plead guilty, despite being innocent of the offence with which they are charged. The recidivist is particularly vulnerable, but everyone is at risk.[4] The following examples (which are fairly representative of the 33 cases in this group) indicate some of the main factors that give rise to this dilemma:

Case 2: The barrister said, 'I'm not going to advise you to plead guilty to something you didn't do, but the way it's going you're going to be found guilty and you'll get a bigger sentence for wasting the court's time.'

Case 87: The barrister turned around and says, 'There are six or eight policemen who are going to stand up in court and say you did assault the police. For us to turn around and call them liars is not on. The jury are bound to take the law's word for it, rather than a well-known criminal unless we have strong evidence, a witness who has no record to prove it.'

Case 110: It had got me down, I was that worried about it. I kept worrying about how long I was going to get and in the finish I just thought 'Well, blow it—I'm not going to have no more adjournments, I'm not going to have no more anxiety of coming up here and then having to go home again and come back again. I'm going to get it over and done with. I'll take my chances and see what happens.'

Case 125: The barrister turned round and says, 'If I were you, I'd forget my pride. I know you think you're innocent but if you're proved guilty, I think you'll go down—I can't guarantee it but I think you will.' Then I said, 'I don't want to do bloody time for something I haven't done' and he says 'We can get it all sorted out.' So in the end, I turned round and said 'Well, I'm here for your advice, I'll also accept it.' He was very nice—he didn't try to force me, it was just his advice. I mean if you've got somebody like that as your counsel, you're a mug not to take their advice. That's the way I looked upon it, so I pleaded guilty.

Case 144: I was fed up. I was losing that much time off work I was frightened I'd get the sack. I've got the house

66

and the mortgage. You work out how many times I was at the Magistrates [before being committed for trial], how many months it went over before I was finally convicted. At the time it was a worrying thing, it was worrying for months and months—it just got over boiling point and that was it.

These few examples, which are themselves greatly truncated accounts of the factors that led the defendants in question to plead guilty, could easily be multiplied and, if the stories related to us by defendants bear *some* resemblance to the truth, a very disturbing situation is disclosed. Any system of administering justice that could induce innocent individuals in anything like these numbers to plead guilty could not be tolerated. We do not know, of course, whether the defendants in question were in fact innocent, but their stories, a good many of which appeared convincing, call for a careful examination of the possibility of innocent men pleading guilty.

We have described in previous chapters how the pressures and inducements that defendants related may on occasions be intense. Even accepting that, it is arguable that no inducement could be so attractive and no threat sufficiently grave to cause an innocent man to plead guilty. There are two main answers to this. First, the inducement or threat is not made in the abstract; it is made to the defendant when he is in an uncomfortable and tense situation isolated from his friends and unsure of what is best to do. Deprived of the advice of those he trusts, he feels he is being asked by counsel to choose between two, and only two, alternatives, neither of which is palatable. If the only alternative open to the defendant is between probation and prison, or between a short term of imprisonment and a long term of imprisonment, the choice is clear, even for an innocent man. Second, and crucially, the defendant's plea is not primarily determined by the accuracy of the charges laid against him; in the majority of cases the defendant enters a plea of guilty because he believes that he will probably or certainly be convicted at trial and given a much heavier sentence for contesting the case. It is his expectation of what will happen to him if he pleads not guilty that causes him to enter a guilty plea. Although, therefore, it is possible to list factors that might cause an innocent man to plead guilty,[5] it is more important to examine those factors that give rise to this fatalistic perception.

One factor of great importance is the strength and nature of the evidence against the accused. In the vast majority of cases in our sample, the evidence in the prosecution's case disclosed at the least a *prima facie* case against the defendant. In many of these cases, however, the most damaging evidence consisted in verbal admissions attributed to the defendant or a statement signed by him. No fewer than 49 defendants (40 per cent) in the sample alleged that the police had falsely attributed to them verbal statements they did not make (known universally by defendants as 'verbals'), and of the 57 who claimed innocence, a third made such allegations.[6] Our interviews contain an extensive catalogue of alleged fabrication of evidence and, to a lesser extent, police brutality. The allegations, some credible, some less so, span the spectrum: illiterates being duped into signing statements the contents of which turn out to be different from what they were led to believe; the weak and inexperienced being 'helped' to compile a statement, highly damaging to the accused but not realised to be so at the time of signing; verbal admissions being fabricated; and threats or violence used to persuade defendants into signing statements. We have no way of verifying these allegations though many were convincingly put forward and frequently made with no obvious sense of grievance. Indeed, it was common for those who had been arrested on earlier occasions to qualify allegations by saying that they were 'treated better than the last time' and that 'at least I wasn't slapped about this time'; they are satisfied if they were treated less badly on this occasion than on other occasions in the past. In many ways this attitude to the police is one of the most depressing features emerging from defendants' accounts—the fatalistic resignation to a very bad lot.

Few defendants in this sample knew what their rights were at the police station. Earlier research by Zander (1972a) showed that over half of defendants in his sample of appellants did not attempt to contact a solicitor when interviewed at the police station and, of those who did ask to see one, almost three-quarters were refused. The situation in Birmingham is even more unfavourable. 70 per cent of defendants, because of ignorance or some other reason, said they did not ask to see a solicitor while being interviewed by the police. Of those who said they had made such a request, no fewer than six out of every seven said that they were not allowed to. Four defendants stated that they had arrived at the police station in the first instance with a solicitor and only five others said that they were allowed to see a solicitor when they made their request, and three of these were only permitted to do so after prior interrogation lasting some hours. Only six defendants, out of 121 interviewed, said that a solicitor was present while they were being questioned at the police station. To many defendants bad treatment at the police station is accepted uncritically only because they expect from previous encounters even worse treatment.

The importance of police verbals in this context is that their force is never spent until after sentence. If the defendant wishes to challenge a statement or verbal allegations in court, his barrister will often quickly make clear that this is impossible or, at least, that it is a course so fraught with danger that it must not be undertaken. Although, therefore, many defendants believe when they arrive at the Crown Court that they have successfully resisted pressures from the police to plead guilty, this belief is shattered by their barrister. He will as a rule point out that the police evidence will invariably be preferred to that of the defendant, that the defendant must avoid 'mud-slinging' and that an attack on police witnesses may well annoy the judge and lead to a much heavier sentence. It is comparatively easy for counsel to convince recidivists of the folly of challenging police verbals or a statement, but first offenders are also relatively easily persuaded. That counsel may well be prudent in giving this advice—indeed it has been put to us that counsel *must* give this advice—is in itself a demonstration of a grave weakness in the criminal justice system as it at present operates. As we shall argue in chapter

6, the inability of counsel, or for that matter anyone else working within the adversarial system, accurately to determine the truth of what took place during the defendant's interrogation at the police station, inevitably colours the sort of advice he can realistically give his client. One result is that the defendant is convinced of the hopelessness of his position, so that all thought of being acquitted evaporates. He is, in short, resigned to making the best of a bad lot, even to pleading guilty though he believes himself to be innocent.

A second and related factor, inducing in the defendant a fatalistic attitude, is the advice he receives from his barrister about his prospects of being acquitted or convicted should he contest the case. Where the subject was raised, the defendant invariably stated that his barrister had made it clear that there was no real prospect of an acquittal at trial. On the face of it, this is a rather strange situation, for one of the criticisms levelled at juries has been the high rate of acquittal and the unpredictability of the verdict.[7] Yet counsel in our cases is convinced, or rather convinces the defendant, that a conviction at trial is a virtual certainty. Indeed, according to the defendants we interviewed, barristers hardly ever mentioned the jury in pre-trial discussions: all the conversation focused on the sentence and the judge. Although we anticipated that counsel might raise the subject of trial by jury with the defendant in terms of it being something of a lottery, it appears that jury trial was scarcely discussed by counsel in these terms at all. In consequence, the defendant tends more readily to accept counsel's view that the best course is to arrange the plea in such a way that a lesser sentence will result.

It seems, then, that this attack on the defendant's intention to plead not guilty, coupled with the offer of a deal and a light sentence, or the risk of a heavier sentence if the advice is ignored, or the hints that the judge will be lenient, were very effective in weakening the resolve of most defendants in this sample to plead not guilty. A few illustrations demonstrate this clearly:

Case 146 [a recidivist]: I pleaded not guilty right up to the Crown and the barrister came down to see me and said, 'I've read these police statements and I don't think you've got much chance going not guilty against these.' Well I said I couldn't see why not because there were a lot of things which could have been challenged. He said, 'Look at these, read these police statements.' Well, they were a load of verbal, know what I mean, lies like. The barrister said that as soon as I turn round and say that it wasn't true what they said in their statements, then my character could be brought before the jury, which wouldn't look too good. So I had no chance that way, because I've been done quite a few times before. I saw the solicitor three weeks before I came up for trial and I pointed out things in the police statements I'd like challenged. But when I came up to court, nothing had been checked up, nothing had been challenged. So I thought it was pointless. The barrister didn't seem to have any faith in me. I mean they need to have faith in you to do any good, and he had no faith at all. If I'd had a good barrister I'd have pleaded not guilty, because all it was was police verbals. I was not guilty really but, there you are, know what I mean?

Case 148 [a young middle-class first offender present at a stag party in which a violent fracas occurred]: The police took me to the police station and said that I must make a statement. They were quite insistent so I made a statement. The police were quite friendly with me really; they tried to make whatever I said in the statement best for me. What I said was put down in the statement but it said in the statement that I had done it, hit [the victim] with a glass. At the time I made the statement I didn't know whether I had done it or not and it wasn't until the next morning that I realised that it was not me who had used the glass. They never told me the seriousness of the charge at the police station. I was kept in a freezing cell so I kept waking up every time my body temperature dropped. I kept asking for a cup of tea, because on films you see them giving you cups of tea, but they never gave me a cup. Before I made the statement the sergeant told me I had to admit to it. When I saw my solicitor I told him I hadn't used the glass, because I hadn't and he told me 'Obviously this other bloke [the defendant's co-accused] is the villain of the piece but you have got to plead guilty because of your statement. It's the law, not what's right.' He kept constantly saying, 'What can we do? You have admitted it in your statement.' I kept telling him what really happened, the truth, and so did the witnesses but he did not seem to be interested. When I saw the barrister on the day of the trial he said, 'You must plead guilty because you've admitted it in the statement.' He said he entirely believed my story but I must plead guilty as I'd be found guilty anyway. I was innocent but they just depressed me with all this talk of being found guilty anyway, so I just did what I was told. It's all right being a martyr and going to court and saying you didn't do it, which I didn't, but you can't risk it when the barrister and solicitor say you're going to get found guilty. What can be right about that? You have to go along with them.

It is of course possible that defence counsel convinces the defendant of the hopelessness of his position only in those cases where a conviction at trial *is* certain; where the balance of evidence is such that no reasonable jury could possibly acquit. If this were so, then the procedure of negotiated justice outside the court-room might be said to be an effective filter, ridding the trial system of hopeless cases. The difficulties involved in evaluating the accuracy of the bargaining system in this respect are enormous and, in consequence, commentators have tended instead to focus on the propriety of the negotiating procedure. As Folberg (1968) put it:

Whether or not more innocent men may be convicted because of plea bargains as compared to trial should, however, not be the central question. Because the accuracy of the result can not be guaranteed by either method the appropriateness of the method becomes as important as the outcome. [p. 203]

We are, however, in a position to evaluate to some extent at least the probability of conviction had the case been contested. The evidence from our study suggests to us that the system we have described operates in only a crude way and that the injustices it brings about are both frequent and profound. As described earlier, we were given copies of all committal papers

72

in the sample by the Crown Court authorities and these were independently examined by two experts (a retired Justices' Clerk and a retired Chief Constable) who gave their opinions of the likelihood of a case ending in a conviction or an acquittal, and indicated in addition the degree of certainty (as measured on a five-point scale) with which they expected this outcome. In those cases for which they predicted an acquittal, they expressed a view about whether or not the prosecution was justified. As will be clear from the discussion that follows, they also added forthright and provocative views about individual cases.

The predictions made by the two assessors are not in any sense to be taken as validations or refutations of an individual's claim to be innocent. Since our assessors based their predictions on the prosecution case as it was set out in the committal papers, they were unable as a rule to form any accurate impression of, say, whether defendants were likely to say that they had been verballed by the police or else whether the statements they had signed had been extracted by improper methods. Establishing that the prosecution is likely to prove its case is a different exercise from judging a man to be innocent or guilty. But insofar as our assessors commented upon the likelihood of the prosecution succeeding in a particular case, the exercise allows the possibility of determining the extent to which a defendant was justified in claiming that he was entitled to be tried by jury, and provides an independent assessment of the likelihood of conviction or acquittal at trial based upon the strength of the case for the prosecution. Since our assessors, in making their predictions, were in almost all cases relying upon the same evidence as counsel had before him in advising the defendant,[8] their statements provide an independent check upon whether there was sufficient evidence against the defendant to warrant a guilty plea.

Perhaps not surprisingly, in most of the cases our assessors were of the view that there was a strong likelihood that the defendant would be convicted at trial. In no fewer than 79 per cent of cases, both assessors predicted a conviction with some certainty. For these cases, then, the evidence against the defendant was extremely strong, so strong that, had the prosecution witnesses come up to proof (which can by no means be guaranteed), the probable result would have been a conviction. If, in such cases, counsel indicated this to the defendant and then advised a plea of guilty, no criticism could be levelled at the propriety of such advice; indeed, in this limited sense, the final decision to plead guilty may well be viewed as a prudent one.

In the remaining 21 per cent of cases, our assessors expressed uncertainty as to the likely outcome or even thought an acquittal likely. In many of these cases the defendant had himself claimed innocence during the course of our interview. It is noteworthy that the predictors had strong words to say about the strength of the prosecution case in these examples and, in the quotes that follow, we cite only those comments of the predictors that relate to cases in which the defendant also protested his innocence to us in his interview.[9]

[*Case 55*, in which both assessors predicted an acquittal]: The jury are likely to conclude that the accused had no intention of stealing or keeping the articles. The police officer who stopped the defendant was precipitate in making an arrest. The charge might well have been refused by the officer in charge at the police station. The charge may be dismissed without calling on the defence.

[*Case 68*, in which both assessors predicted an acquittal on the charge to which the defendant pleaded guilty and of which he claimed to be innocent. The defendant's own statement is cited earlier in this chapter.]: I see no evidence to support any of the charges against this accused. It may be that the absence of his co-defendant has weakened this case and I suspect that, in his absence, we are playing Hamlet without the Prince.

[*Case 97*, in which both assessors very strongly predicted an acquittal and felt that the decision to prosecute was unjustified]: There is a complete absence of evidence to support either the charge of taking the car or of stealing from the car ... There is a faint possibility that the jury will convict because of his statement but it is unlikely.

[*Case 138*, in which the defendant pleaded guilty to conspiracy]: I think that this case will not get off the ground. I have never read such inconsequential evidence. Taken in the context of the case as a whole, I do not consider that there was any offence committed. Probably the accused is a nuisance and the complainant had been promised police assistance. I consider that the time of the court should not be taken up with this rubbish.

We do not cite these examples in order to exaggerate the extent to which our assessors' view of the likely outcome of a case was palpably at variance with what counsel appears to have believed, and we re-emphasise the fact that in four cases out of five our assessors' view of the case was not substantially different from counsel's in this respect. The above examples do, however, suggest that on occasions defendants' protestations of innocence may have been too lightly disregarded by counsel. Moreover, in a few cases, as is clear from the comments we have cited, the view of our experienced assessors was that a conviction was not only unlikely but the evidence in the prosecution's case was so weak that the charge should not have been brought in the first place. Yet in these cases, as well as in cases where the prosecution evidence was strong, pressures of an irresistible nature to plead guilty were apparently brought to bear upon several defendants. It is important here to mention the preliminary analysis of almost 1,000 predictions made in relation to cases in both Birmingham and London in which the defendant pleaded not guilty. This analysis has shown that, when the assessors said that the prosecution of a case was not justified, over 80 per cent resulted in acquittals. This seems to us strong evidence to support the contention that certain cases in the present sample (and there are seven in which the assessors said that the prosecution was not justified) would have ended in acquittals had the cases gone to trial. For those other cases in which the assessors thought the prosecution justified but nonetheless predicted an acquittal, it is arguable that their views were sometimes over-optimistic and that, had the defendant pleaded not guilty, he would nevertheless have been convicted at trial. We shall never know. But at the very least we can state that many defendants said they pleaded guilty under pressure despite the fact that they claimed to be innocent. In many of these cases the prosecution evidence was weak and it is our view that they ought to have been allowed to have had their cases determined by a jury. We have already referred in chapter 3 to the practice of certain defence counsel taking upon themselves the function of the jury in deciding whether a defendant who asserts his innocence is guilty or not.[10] It is important to note, in this context, that even when our assessors anticipated that a particular defendant was likely to be convicted, their comments often clearly imply that the issue is best left to the jury to decide.[11] The following comments are typical of those commonly expressed by them in this regard:

> The jury will have the advantage of seeing the two parties and hearing their evidence being tested under cross-examination. [*Case 20*]

> Much may depend on the cross-examination of the defendant and his witnesses. The jury may give him the benefit of the doubt. [*Case 25*]

> There is a *prima facie* case of burglary which should be settled by a trial. [*Case 37*]

> It is a question of whether the jury will believe the defendant's story or, at least, give him the benefit of the doubt. They may find it implausible. [*Case 40*]

> I consider that there is a fair chance that the jury will find that the accused did not undertake retention of the goods for the benefit of his co-accused but took them from his house in panic after he knew of his co-accused's arrest. [*Case 43*]

> The jury are likely to accept that he acted in self-defence. [*Case 61*]

> It is doubtful how the jury will regard this affair. The victim was provocative and the jury may feel that she asked for a blow. Much will depend on the impression they make on the jury. [*Case 64*]

> The probability is that the jury will believe the victim and

his witness. The possibility is that they will believe the accused. [*Case 82*]

The jury may have difficulty in believing either the accused or his self-confessed accomplice. [*Case 94*]

The failure of the victim to identify the accused may influence the decision of the jury but the circumstantial evidence is strong. [*Case 99*]

The jury may well come to the conclusion that there was a free fight with all equally to blame. There is some doubt as to how the victim came by his injuries. There is some evidence to put to the jury. [*Case 122*]

These comments do not necessarily indicate that our assessors would have disagreed with the advice that counsel gave to the defendants in question; taking our assessors' view of the likely outcome, together with the fact that many defendants admitted their involvement in the offences charged in the course of interviews with us, supports the view that in a majority of cases the final result may well have been realistic, expedient and prudent, though we are ourselves unhappy about the way this result is arrived at in some of the cases. The comments cited above do, however, suggest that, though often the defendant's chances may be slim, the issue is nonetheless contentious. In such cases, it is not by any means unreasonable of the defendant to seek to have it settled in court rather than hastily outside it. The assessors' comments in many of the cases suggest that it would be quite indefensible to disregard the defendant's expressed intention to plead not guilty and go for trial.

Another telling indication of the somewhat cursory treatment many defendants complained about is to be found outside this sample of cases where it is at least arguable that the defendants concerned may well have been convicted, and more severely sentenced, had the case been allowed to go before a jury. We have, as part of our separate study of jury trials, interviewed defendants tried by jury over a twenty-month period in 1975 and 1976. The interviews with these defendants followed broadly similar lines to those interviews dealt with in this book. In addition to the interviews conducted with defendants, we have been able to obtain the views of judges, solicitors and police officers about the outcome of 500 contested trials. It emerges from this part of the research that it sometimes happens in Birmingham that defendants who are acquitted at trial nevertheless appear to be subject to the same kinds of pressures to plead guilty as described in chapters 2 and 3 of this book. The opinions expressed to us about the outcome of some of these cases by judges, police officers and solicitors were that the defendants concerned were rightly acquitted and, in a few cases, the police accepted that the defendant was in fact innocent.[12] The following are extracts from the interviews conducted with these defendants:

Case A: Three times before the court the barrister said, 'This judge is a bad judge, he's one who sends them down. Plead guilty and you'll get a suspended sentence and a fine; plead not guilty and you'll go down. He's one of them sort of judges ...' My barrister was a great bloke even though he tried to pressure me. Later on [when I had been acquitted] he said he was very glad he didn't persuade me to change my plea—and that's good enough for me—I couldn't speak too highly of him.[13]

Case B: The barrister advised me to plead guilty. He said it would really be better for me because the person who had done it said all of us had 'egged' him on. The barrister said I'd be better off if I pleaded guilty—I'd either get a suspended sentence or a very light prison sentence. He told me he thought it might go hard for me if I was found guilty—he meant that I would certainly go to prison ... Apart from advising me to plead guilty he was very good and spoke up for me in court very well.

Case C: The barrister tried to get my wife to persuade me to plead guilty, but I wouldn't. When I told him that the police were lying, he said that we couldn't have any mud-slinging in court. I was upset that he didn't seem to believe I was innocent.

Case D: When it came to discussing the plea, the barrister said, 'You want to start thinking about your wife a bit— and you want to plead guilty. The evidence against you is overwhelming—I can see your version of it, there's two sides to every story. It's going to be hard to make out that 11 police officers are lying—I know you know they're lying but, let's be honest about it, proving it is a different thing. I think it would be better if you went upstairs now and plead guilty to all three charges. If you do that, I think you'll get three or four years.' So I said, 'No—I'm not going to throw my hands up to that.' He said, 'Well, if you don't, you'll end up with six or seven years.' I said I'd rather do six or seven years as a matter of principle. He said, 'Why don't you think about your wife and kids?' I said, 'I am, that's why I'm pleading not guilty.'

Case E: The barrister tried to con me into pleading guilty. He said, 'Your chances don't seem very good. To tell you the truth, you haven't got a chance and you should plead guilty. If you plead guilty, I can work it that you get a suspended sentence or a heavy fine.' All three times I saw him he said to plead guilty.

Case F: The barrister tried to get me to change my plea—I don't know why. I certainly wasn't going to plead guilty to something I hadn't done. He told me I'd get a lighter sentence. I've read in the press recently that barristers try to get people to plead guilty to get the case over quickly, which to me isn't the thing. This happened during the trial after the first two days. He got me and M [co-defendant] and his barrister in one room and said, 'Look, we think you ought to plead guilty.' Frankly I came out of that room rather annoyed really, because I'm not going to plead guilty to something I'm not guilty of. I certainly didn't see it as very good advice.

It is clear, therefore, that several defendants who are ultimately acquitted at trial (some of whom have no criminal record whatsoever) may have had to resist before trial strong pressures from counsel to plead guilty. It must be said, nevertheless, that this is a comparatively rare occurrence, for the vast majority of defendants acquitted at trial in our main study were not subjected to such pressures. That it does occasionally happen, however, reinforces our contention that, within the sample of 121 defendants, there are a number who may well have been innocent, wholly or in part, yet who were induced to plead guilty and suffered considerably, both personally and socially, as a result.[14] There are others in addition who, if not innocent, were likely to have found the prosecution unable to prove its case at trial and who would therefore have been acquitted. There are, it is true, dangers in overstating the precision of trial by jury. Our own research on this question (which is still in progress at the time of writing) has identified a number of disturbing cases where the defendant was convicted when, in the opinion of a majority of those who have expressed views to us on the outcome, he ought instead to have been acquitted.[15] We would argue, however, that, notwithstanding the inaccuracies of jury trial, the number of serious miscarriages of justice it produces is, in numerical terms at least, of slight significance compared to that produced by the system of negotiated justice we have described.

NOTES AND REFERENCES

1. Dell writes, for instance:
   Whatever weight may be put on the women's accounts in these cases, the point which repeatedly emerged was the importance to the accused person of having legal advice before pleading ... Two-thirds of the unrepresented women who maintained that they were innocent nevertheless pleaded guilty, while among those who were represented, whether in the higher or lower courts, the percentage pleading inconsistently was not more than 15 per cent [p. 35].
2. On this point, see Oppenheim (1966) ch. 3.
3. Christie (1977) makes the following perceptive observation:
   Lawyers are particularly good at stealing conflicts. They are trained for it. They are trained to prevent and solve conflicts. They are socialised into a sub-culture with a surprisingly high agreement concerning interpretation of norms and regarding what sort of information can be accepted as relevant in each case. Many among us have, as laymen, experienced the sad moments of truth when our lawyers tell us that our best arguments in our fight against our neighbour are without any legal relevance whatsoever and that we for God's sake ought to keep quiet about them in court. Instead they pick out arguments we might find irrelevant or even wrong to use. [p. 4]
4. Rosett (1967) states this proposition as follows:
   Stated in absurd terms, if the choice is between pleading guilty and paying the man the two dollars, or being tried, convicted and sentenced to hang, few would choose to contest the case, no matter how innocent they might be. [p. 73]

80

5. For a discussion of these factors see, for instance, Dash (1951) pp. 393–5; Alschuler (1968) p. 60; Newman and NeMoyer (1970) pp. 393–4; Thomas (1974) pp. 305–6; Ferguson and Roberts (1974) pp. 542–6; Gallagher (1974); Finkelstein (1975).

6. Again it is important to note that no questions were included in the questionnaire relating to this matter. All such allegations were volunteered by the defendant in his interview.

7. The most widely publicised view on this is that of Sir Robert Mark, former Metropolitan Police Commissioner, as stated in the 1973 Dimbleby lecture. Figures reproduced in McCabe and Purves (1972b) indicate that defendants in many parts of the country are more likely to be acquitted than convicted if tried by jury.

8. Though not, of course, having the benefit of speaking to the defendant himself, of seeing the defence brief or of studying the defendant's antecedents.

9. We shall not distinguish in the quotes between the two assessors, and, for some of the cases examined, the opinions of both assessors are cited.

10. As one defendant put it, in *Case 45*:

There's no justice. It's just barristers getting their fees—not knowing about their clients, asking them to plead guilty. They all work together and try to guess who is guilty and who is not guilty, without trying you first. It shouldn't all be settled beforehand.

11. As noted in chapter 1, the assessors were sent committal statements relating to all likely contested cases and they had no way of knowing which of these were to be tried by jury and which were not. In most cases, neither had we nor, for that matter, the defendants themselves.

12. In these cases, one of our assessors also predicted, with a high degree of certainty, that the defendants concerned would be acquitted.

13. The police officer, interviewed about the outcome of this trial, made the following interesting comment:

Although he got charged with X, not for one minute was it anything to do with him and he was too scared to say anything against X. I should have found out that he was on holiday at the time the offence was committed. My own fault. It was the best possible verdict from our point of view [since X was convicted].

14. It would be a mistake to assume that, by pleading guilty and presumably receiving a more lenient sentence from the court, the defendants in this sample were able to avoid the more serious consequences of trial and conviction. This is very far from being so and it may well be the case that those who plead guilty and stridently maintain their innocence suffered more than others in the sample. Many were sent to prison, or lost their jobs or in other ways experienced considerable upheaval to their lives. In terms of the sentences they received, half had received custodial sentences, which is a higher proportion than that found for the sample as a whole. Our independent assessors predicted acquittals, sometimes jointly, in 18 cases in which interviews were conducted, and of these eight defendants were given custodial sentences. In a further nine cases, the assessors expressed considerable uncertainty about whether the prosecution would succeed or not, and of these defendants (five of whom

claimed to be innocent, wholly or in part of the charges they faced) four had received custodial sentences.

15. Brandon and Davies (1973) discuss a number of cases of wrongful imprisonment in some detail. Other researchers have discussed the question of the perversity of jury acquittals, and all such studies identify a small number of cases in which an apparently indefensible acquittal was returned by the jury. On this latter point see particularly Kalven and Zeisel (1966); McCabe and Purves (1972b); Zander (1974).

5   BY-PASSING THE DEFENDANT

Much has been written in recent years about the difficulties encountered by the unrepresented defendant appearing in the criminal courts. The procedure of the court will probably be foreign to him and he will not be able precisely to anticipate what will happen next as all others involved in almost any court-room drama can.[1] He is unlikely to be able to understand in more than a superficial way what is taking place, let alone engage effectively in the complex business of cross-examination that is at the heart of Anglo-American adversarial confrontation. Some have seen legal representation as almost a panacea to these problems, yet paradoxically one of the most immediately striking findings to emerge from our interviews with defendants, all of whom were legally represented, was their profound sense of non-involvement in, if not complete alienation from, the legal process in which they had been concerned.

This is by no means easy to quantify, particularly because the defendant himself is often absorbed and co-opted into the machinery of justice itself and may well in consequence regard the judicial system in a surprisingly uncritical light. Bottoms and McClean (1976) in their study of defendants note that 'in many cases defendants simply did not "take decisions" in any formal sense' (p. 8) and, within our sample of cases, there were many defendants who were, for instance, confused even about who had decided that their case would be tried at the Crown Court. Such defendants had been quite happy as a rule to entrust the case to their legal advisers and had blindly followed their advice. They assumed that counsel would know what was

83

best and safeguard their interests.[2] Others received the advice of their lawyers somewhat more critically but, as earlier chapters have demonstrated, they felt unable in the end to resist the pressures or inducements that were held out. It is perhaps not surprising, then, that almost half of all the defendants we interviewed felt that they had not themselves made the final decision as to plea and that this decision had in effect been taken by their legal advisers.[3] Those conducting the interviews in each case made an independent assessment of this question in the light of what the defendant had said in the course of the interview and it appeared to us that at least three-quarters of the defendants had in reality allowed the barrister to make the final decision for them.

There is no doubt that very many barristers had the best interests of their clients at heart and that the advice they gave was realistic and honest. But equally it appeared to us that, in a minority of cases, the conduct of counsel was misguided and even, on occasion, unethical. In such cases, the safeguards encapsulated in what is known in America as 'due process of law' seemed to have been infringed by the defendant's own barrister. None of these observations would be surprising to anyone acquainted with the American literature on the role of defence counsel in negotiating pleas of guilty.[4] It has been customary in America to refer to the 'co-optation' of the legal and other court personnel into what Blumberg (1967) has described as 'an organised system of complicity' whereby 'the patterned, covert, informal breaches, and evasion of "due process" are institutionalised, but are, nevertheless, denied to exist'.[5] The defendant is seen by Blumberg to be outside the network of intimate relationships that comprise the court, and, significantly, the specific objectives of the other actors are seen as by no means necessarily concordant with those of the defendant. Indeed, their interests may well conflict with his. The career interests of counsel, as several American commentators have argued, in such a system are likely to be adversely affected if he fails to maintain good relations with the prosecutor, and one way to achieve such relations is to demonstrate a willingness to engage in bargains

84

over plea. In this way, it is almost inevitable that the interests of the client will be of only secondary importance.[6] The defendant is relatively powerless in this situation—in many cases, a refusal to comply is his only weapon. That defendants feel in such circumstances an acute sense of frustration and alienation is not then surprising. Though we do not argue that such an organised system of relationships exists in this form in England, there are a number of parallels between the two jurisdictions. Defendants commonly observed that they had found it difficult to decide whose side their barrister was on, so closely involved did he appear to be with the prosecution.[7] Many more felt they were not genuine parties to what took place in the court or to the decisions that were taken before it. The following quotations illustrate the sense of estrangement expressed by a majority of defendants:

Case 29: The fellow who's prosecuting and the fellow who's defending are not really interested in me. One is looking over the notes of the other as he's going along, to make sure he doesn't make any mistakes. After all, they're near enough mates in the same play. They're the cast of the play, you're just the casual one-day actor. It's just another day's work to them.

Case 82: Everything in the bloody machinery of the court is against you from the start—say, the judge's attitude, the judge's expressions and things. I'm the guy in the middle and who's bothered about me? I've often thought that, from the accused's point of view, it's like a guy on a desert island, with all the little sharks coming in for a little nibble. By God, it's a very, very bad system. It stinks to high heaven. Everything's stacked against the accused ... I had an argument with my barrister about who was going to be called as witnesses and who wasn't —they didn't want to call anyone as witnesses. He refused to ask lots of questions owing to the fact that he's one of the flag wavers. I don't know whether he wants to be a Q.C. or what. I was just dissatisfied with them all in general—putting it bluntly, they all basically piss in the same pot.

Case 148: I never made any decisions, they were all taken

85

for me. I felt like I wasn't controlling things with the solicitor and barrister; I was just being dragged along. I just had no say in what was happening, I was just carried along on the tide of what they said. I had to follow a set route all the way through. I couldn't say 'No, I don't want to go that way', the way it was put there was only one route to follow. It's just like a blind-folded man being guided through a maze; I had to go but I wasn't sure where I was going.

This sense of non-involvement in the pre-trial discussions is often felt even more acutely when the case reaches court. The procedure followed in the Crown Court where there is a plea of guilty is in general straightforward and speedy. The defendant is brought into the dock and the proper officer asks him his name. Assuming that the defendant is the person named in the indictment, the indictment is read to him, or the substance of it stated, and he is asked to plead to it. Counsel for the prosecution then gives an outline of the facts and calls the police officer in charge of the case to give the defendant's antecedent history, detailing his home and educational background, employment and criminal record if any. Counsel for the defence is then given an opportunity to say something in mitigation to the court after which the judge proceeds to sentence. The whole procedure rarely takes more than an hour and is frequently completed in under thirty minutes. The simplicity and speed of these proceedings and the relative lack of critical investigation by commentators of this aspect of the criminal process might seem to indicate that few matters of concern are here raised. This is very far from being the case. The simple and expeditious nature of the proceedings masks a situation in which matters of fundamental importance to sentencing are often neither adequately ventilated nor properly established: some are never raised, some glossed over, and yet others ignored or even deliberately suppressed. In the discussion that follows, we shall describe some of the ways in which defendants perceive the court proceedings following a guilty plea.

Corresponding to the sense of alienation that defendants

experienced in relation to decisions taken before the trial, it is interesting that very many of them described a profound feeling of powerlessness once the decision to plead guilty had been taken and the case presented in open court. Many felt that they were mere spectators in court with decisions being taken about their future as if in their absence. The matter had been in effect delegated to defence counsel, who seemed very much part of the court organisation. The whole ceremony often became in consequence distant and unreal. Many defendants believed that they were not allowed to intervene in the proceedings. The following comments illustrate these sentiments.

> *Case 1*: It felt like listening to a conversation at the trial. They were all talking to each other and I just seemed to be watching and listening. I thought I'd have to speak but I didn't. It was like watching a press conference on the television.

> *Case 34*: I thought it was a bloody farce. I never had a chance to speak my piece. I was just sitting there like a dummy. I couldn't have given a damn—I couldn't have said anything anyway, they were doing all the talking. I didn't care what they did to me in the end.

> *Case 83*: They were discussing why I'd done it and the provocation before I'd even pleaded guilty. It was all being discussed as if I wasn't there.

One matter that contributed to the feeling of alienation of many defendants was the perceived inadequacy of the court proceedings as a means of establishing the facts of the case for the purpose of sentence. There has in fact been a growing recognition recently of the difficulties for the sentencer inherent in cases where a guilty plea is entered.[8] A defendant can be properly sentenced only for what he is proved to have done, but in many cases it is not clear what it has been proved that he did even where there is a plea of guilty. The defendant may wish, for example, to plead guilty to the offence charged but, at the same time, challenge the prosecution's version of the commission of the crime. Only thorough enquiry by the court can clarify such matters; the guilty plea itself is inadequate to make such discriminations.[9] It is clear, however, to any observer of the court system that such enquiry is rarely undertaken with sufficient care. As D. A. Thomas (1970) has written:

> Existing procedures directed to establishing an account of the facts of the offence for the purposes of sentencing are one of the weakest links in our system of criminal procedure ... [p. 80]

The interviews we have conducted with defendants in this sample provide considerable support for this view. Where the defendant has pleaded guilty to an offence or count of which he claims to be innocent, then it is obvious that his version of the circumstances surrounding the alleged offence will be opposed to that given in court. There is little point here in recounting further examples of this sort of case. Frequently, however, the defendant admitted guilt or at the least involvement in the acts constituting the offence. In many such cases, the defendant complained strongly that the account of the offence given to the judge at the sentencing stage was inaccurate. This factual inaccuracy was attributed by defendants to four main causes.

In the first place, some defendants claimed that victims had, for one reason or another, exaggerated the amount of property stolen or in other ways distorted the nature of the offence. Within the present sample, three defendants, all separately charged with offences of theft, said that the victims had reported some property as stolen that was not among the items taken. Thus in *Case 73*:

> We went down for a drink and we decided to do some jobs, some burglaries. We went to a mate's flat and he told us the man in the school flat opposite was away on holiday. So we broke in and took some stuff. On the theft charge I wanted to plead not guilty because, although I had done the job, there was a lot of things they said we had took which we didn't. They said there was £400 took in cash and we never took it; there was no money there. They said there was a film projector and a tape recorder we took, but all we

took was a clock and the telly. I wanted to plead not guilty to show all this.

The defendant ventured the explanation that the victim had reported items missing which had never been in the flat in order to make an excessive claim on the insurance company.

Secondly, a more frequent complaint was that the police had failed to give a proper account of the crime, in that they had placed too much reliance upon the victim's story. Defendants involved in offences of violence against the person were particularly aggrieved about what they saw as a biased picture being presented to the court. These offences were commonly preceded by some heated verbal altercation in which the victim may have precipitated the final assault by some act of provocation, but the defendants felt that the picture presented in court sometimes did not reflect this. Thus, in *Case 103* the defendant pleaded guilty to unlawful wounding having injured the victim in a pub brawl:

There was a row in a public house with a group of Northerners and I was supposed to have hit one of them with a glass. What happened was that there were six of them and two of us and there was a lot of provocation. I was fighting [the victim] and we were rolling about on the floor and his face got cut on broken glass. I told the barrister that I never hit him and that he fell on the glass as we were rolling on the floor but he said, 'You will be found guilty of wounding even if you proved you hadn't actually hit him in the face with the glass.' I argued with him but he told me to plead guilty. As soon as I pleaded guilty there was nothing said on my behalf. When I pleaded guilty they weren't interested any more. They just read out what the police and the Northerners said, and my barrister didn't even mention about the circumstances, so it all sounded a lot worse than it really was. What was said in court, well it might have been a different incident entirely; it wasn't like the actual thing that happened.

The implication of this for sentence was not lost on the defendant. When commenting on the severity of the sentence he had received, he observed:

Judging by what was said in court, the sentence [of $2\frac{1}{2}$ years imprisonment] was probably fair. On the way the judge heard it, he was fair; but he heard a different incident to what happened—even I didn't recognise it as what happened.

A similar point was made by a youth in *Case 99* who pleaded guilty to robbery, having threatened and struck the victim a blow in the course of theft:

The prosecution outlined the offence in court in an exaggerated way. The way the prosecution put this case over, I'd half kicked this bloke to death. If the judge believed that, the sentence of 3 years imprisonment was lenient.

A third reason for factual distortion in court was, according to several defendants, statements in court made by defence counsel. In two cases in particular, the veracity of the defendant's story as given to us in an interview was increased by the fact that the distortion he alleged seemed to have operated in his own favour. For instance, the defendant in *Case 44* said of his barrister:

He's got a great legal mind but I don't agree with the way he handled the case. I don't like people telling lies for me in court, well half lies; he exaggerated the way the police dealt with me. The police slapped me about at the police station, mildly until I lashed out and hit one of them. In court the barrister implied that I hadn't really intended to hit the copper when I had.

The defendant in *Case 108*, charged with theft of two cars, was more specific:

The barrister asked me whether I stole the cars because I was short of money. It was the case with the first car, but not with the second. I told the barrister this but he told a lie in court. In court, he said that I stole both cars because I was short of money, which was a lie. I was a bit disgusted with him to tell you the truth.

Although the inaccuracy in both cases was probably not such as to affect the final sentence given, the allegations are serious in nature. It is, of course, the duty of counsel not knowingly to mislead the court and it is quite possible in these cases that the true explanation of the distortion is not that counsel had deliberately misled the court but that he had spent insufficient time discussing the case with the defendant and had in consequence misunderstood his instructions. Whatever the explanation, however, the court was, in the defendant's view, given a distorted account of the circumstances surrounding the commission of the offence.

The final cause of factual inaccuracy, and by far the most prevalent, was, according to defendants, the fabrication of evidence in the form of police verbals. As we have noted in the previous chapter, no fewer than 49 defendants (40 per cent of the sample) alleged that the police had attributed to them verbal statements they did not make. Perhaps surprisingly, this was an even greater source of grievance than alleged police violence. Altogether 25 defendants strongly alleged that they had been subjected to violence of some kind at the police station. The alleged fabrication of evidence takes a number of forms but mostly relates to tricking the defendant into signing a statement that is in part false or, alternatively, wrongly attributing to him oral admissions. A few examples will show the sorts of allegations made:

Case 13: I agreed to make a statement at the police station but I told them I couldn't read or write and asked for my dad to be with me. The police went to my house and told my dad I was in hospital and then came back and told me that he wouldn't come. So I agreed to sign a statement but when they read it out in court it was different from what I'd said.

Case 75: The police simply verballed me up. I was guilty on two charges but it was wrong of the police to make up the rest on the other charges. They were slapping me about at the station but I don't care about that. It was the verbal I complain about.

Case 131: The police were lying from start to finish. Most policemen don't see it as a job, it's a personal vendetta. They must lie, because nobody's going to admit something straight out, not usually, so no policeman has got

91

enough evidence, 100 per cent. So they must lie here and there otherwise they've got no case.

The principal safeguard to the defendant against these four different sources of distortion ought to be his own counsel. Yet many defendants complained that defence counsel spent insufficient time with them prior to the court hearing, was ill-prepared to put in an adequate plea in mitigation, and was frequently not interested in the defendant's account of what led up to his arrest. In short, for most of the cases we have described in this section, counsel appeared to the defendant to have been unable or unwilling to assist the court in arriving at an accurate account of the circumstances of the offence. It might be expected that where the defendant felt himself badly served by counsel he might attempt to advance his own account to the court. This sometimes did happen, but invariably without effect. Thus,

> *Case 4*: I kept trying to interrupt in court but my barrister wouldn't let me. My barrister said afterwards, 'I didn't want you to commit yourself—I knew you'd get a suspended sentence.' But what I want to know is how he knew; there must have been something funny going on.

In the main, however, defendants did not attempt to volunteer information to the court. There appear to have been two main explanations for this. First, many defendants felt, by the time of the court hearing, so far removed from the proceedings that they no longer wished to be a party to what went on. They concluded that no one, not even their advisers, was interested in their version of events and that it was therefore best to let the proceedings take their course as if they were not present. Secondly, many defendants wanted to speak in court and assumed that, at some point, they would be asked if they wished to say anything. There used to be a requirement that a person convicted of felony be asked formally whether he had anything to say why sentence should not be passed. With the abolition of the distinction between felonies and misdemeanours by the Criminal Law Act, 1967, this requirement lapsed. However, the Criminal Law Revision Committee, on whose report (*7th Report*, 1965) the 1967 Act was based, said in this context:

> [W]e think it highly desirable that as a general rule the Judge, before sentencing the accused, should invite him to say anything if he wishes. Clearly this should always be done when the accused is undefended. Even when he is defended, it seems to us desirable that the accused should be invited to add anything to his counsel's address in mitigation if he wishes, although this must remain a matter for the Judge's discretion. A statutory provision would not in our view be necessary or appropriate.

The practice has grown up, however, that the defendant who pleads guilty is almost never asked if he wishes to say anything before sentence is passed. Numerous defendants complained about this: 'I wanted to say something, but I was never asked'; 'I was given no opportunity to speak'; 'I never said anything. I think there is a rule in the Crown Court, isn't there, that you can't say anything these days for yourself?' Our discussions with court officials indicate that a defendant will be asked if he wishes to say anything only if special circumstances exist, as for example where he has not been well represented or is due for a very heavy sentence. In other circumstances, it is considered preferable for counsel to speak on the defendant's behalf and assumed that the guilty plea is at once an indication of remorse and an acceptance of the case for the prosecution. Although lawyers often talk of the defendant 'having his day in court', the truth is that the proceedings are frequently conducted as if the defendant were not present. As Bankowski and Mungham (1976) put it:

> All too often the defendant is left to make of it what he can. No effort is made to bring him in, even on the court's terms. It is taken for granted that he cannot and moreover does not want to understand. He is universally seen as the recipient of whatever is judged to be appropriate for him. [p. 89]

This cursory treatment of the transients in the court system not only reinforces the process of alienation amongst defendants but also often engenders strong feelings of resentment. Nevertheless, it is worth examining whether this feeling of resentment is in part misplaced; whether, despite the sense of non-participation in the court proceedings, defendants (or some of them) do in fact benefit by pleading guilty.

Much has been written in recent years by sociologists and other commentators about the extent to which certain groups of defendants are able to secure the greatest benefits and concessions from any system based on informal negotiation. In this context it is important to examine the extent to which any groups are able to benefit from the system of negotiated justice we have described. Implicit in much of what we have written in earlier chapters has been a deep sense of grievance on the part of very many defendants, and it is certainly the case that the defendants in the sample taken as a whole expressed considerable dissatisfaction at the legal processes they had recently experienced. Less than a quarter could be said to be even broadly satisfied with the standard of justice they had received, in the sense that they voiced no serious criticism of any of the parties with whom they had come into contact. It is a matter of concern that no less than 60 per cent stated explicitly that they were generally or grossly dissatisfied with the treatment they had received. We have already catalogued some of their main sources of dissatisfaction in earlier chapters of this book. Although we can of course never know—and neither can the defendants themselves—what would have been the outcome had they pleaded not guilty instead, some insight into the question of who benefits from the system may be gained by comparing the subjective impressions of different groups of defendants.

We are interested in particular in examining the hypothesis of Newman (1956), and the broadly similar hypothesis of Chambliss (1969) and of other conflict theorists (which in many ways represent the received view in the United States), that the system of negotiated justice benefits the sophisticated professional criminal at the expense of his less sophisticated counterpart. Some writers explain this in terms of the superior knowledge, intelligence and experience of professional criminals; others argue that there exist fundamental and inherent biases in the judicial process that operate very much to the detriment of the naïve, the inarticulate and the powerless.[10] One report discussing the situation in the United States summarises the problem in the following concise way:

> Too often the result [of plea bargaining procedures] may be excessive leniency for professional and habitual criminals who generally have expert legal advice and are best able to take full advantage of the bargaining opportunity. Marginal offenders, on the other hand, may be dealt with harshly, and left with a deep sense of injustice, having learned too late of the possibilities of manipulation offered by the system.[11]

We have been fortunate in this study to have obtained from the police a good deal of information relevant to an examination of this question. Not only have we been able to obtain details from the police about a defendant's formal criminal record, but we have in addition been given information on police suspicions of his criminal activity (whether or not this has been the subject of criminal prosecution), of his skill in crime, of his knowledge of legal rights and the like.[12] We have argued elsewhere that any measure of professionalism that relies on a defendant's criminal record must be regarded as irrelevant and misleading on the grounds that a long criminal record is as likely to be an indication of ineptitude in criminal activity as of professionalism.[13] This is largely borne out by an examination of the information supplied by the police on the professional involvement of this sample of defendants. Only a small minority of recidivists, even those with very long criminal records, were seen by the police as being in any real sense professionals; furthermore, of the 26 defendants in the sample who scored highly on the composite measure of professionalism we used, almost a quarter had never been convicted of any indictable criminal offence.[14]

This group of 26 defendants who represent those towards

the top end of the professionalism continuum, as identified by the police, is of course a good deal broader than that hard-core of serious professional or organised criminals often referred to by the police and commentators as representing a particular threat or danger to the public.[15] What the group of 26 defendants consists of are rather individuals who are suspected by the police of making a fair amount out of crime, who are knowledgeable about their legal rights and who may well be prepared to resort to illegal methods to avoid conviction, and who generally show some degree of skill and sophistication in their criminal activities.[16] There are within this sub-group perhaps a couple of individuals who might be described as representing a serious danger to the public, but it would be quite absurd to characterise the remainder in this way. The concept of 'professional crime' is, as other writers on the subject have argued,[17] a slippery one and of only limited value for descriptive and analytical purposes. The measure used here is only crudely and arbitrarily defined, yet it is very interesting that, when used to test the hypothesis relating to the benefits accruing to professional as compared with other criminals, the results are surprisingly clear-cut. Although it does appear to be the case that a very small number of highly professional criminals did derive considerable benefit from this system of negotiated justice, in the sense that they were able (by delaying their final decision as to plea) to make a strategic decision so as to obtain the maximum concessions from the prosecution, nevertheless, by and large, the great majority of these professional criminals seemed to fare a good deal worse than others in the sample. In this sense, these results provide no support for the hypothesis as stated by Newman or Chambliss. If we examine these 26 cases in greater detail, it stands out clearly that they were, as a group, considerably less satisfied with the treatment they received than others in the sample. Indeed, no fewer than 23 of them said that they were dissatisfied—frequently grossly dissatisfied— with what they had experienced. Often they had good reason to feel this way, and the causes of their widespread disillusionment are not hard to find. The professional group complains more bitterly than the others about the harshness or unfairness of the treatment meted out to them at each stage in the legal process. It may of course be the case that this group was on the whole more critical and demanding than other defendants, but this is not very likely. It seemed to us from the interviews we conducted that they often did receive less favourable treatment from the police, their lawyers and the courts. For instance, on arrest, professionals were over twice as likely as other defendants to say that they had requested a solicitor while being interviewed at the police station, yet all without exception said they were refused permission.[18] A very much higher proportion of these professional defendants expressed strong resentment at the way the police had dealt with them; almost half of them complained strongly of police violence or verbals—and frequently of both. More of them expressed extreme dissatisfaction with the legal advice they had received, complaining more often than other defendants that they had been persuaded against their will to plead guilty, often on the grounds that it would be foolish to attempt to challenge police evidence or verbals. Perhaps surprisingly, fewer of them said they had been offered any identifiable bargain or other inducement to plead guilty. Finally, many more of them (almost 70 per cent) ended up in prison. This is, then, hardly a picture of professional criminals being able to manipulate the legal system to serve their own ends; rather it is a picture of a system in which the dice seem pretty heavily loaded against all defendants but against the professionals in particular.

It is in fact a good deal easier to say who suffers most from the system of informal justice we have described than it is to identify groups of defendants who appeared to have benefited from it. Certainly the recidivists in the sample did not on the whole complain more or less about their experiences than those with few or no prior convictions. Individuals of higher social class did not appear to be more or less satisfied than their lower-class counterparts.[19] Some few defendants charged with particular types of offences found themselves, usually fortuitously, in a relatively strong bargaining position and were able to turn this to their own advantage. The three defendants charged with sexual offences, for instance, benefited from the understandable reluctance of the prosecution to call their victims to give evidence, and thus these defendants were able to strike relatively favourable bargains. But by and large the benefits that may accrue from the system tend to be somewhat random, based more on chance factors than any discernible generalised pattern of advantage.

NOTES AND REFERENCES

1. See the excellent discussion of Bottoms and McClean (1976) pp. 55–7 on this point.
2. As one defendant put it: 'He's got the experience, he's been to college and all that and knows what to do. So when he said it was best to plead guilty, I thought O.K., he's the brains so I went along with it.'
3. In the vast majority of cases, the term 'legal adviser' refers here predominantly to the defendant's barrister. Barristers are on the whole far more influential than solicitors in inducing a defendant to plead guilty. In only twelve of our cases did a solicitor seem to exert heavy pressure on a defendant to plead guilty and the barrister apparently reinforced this advice in no fewer than ten of these cases.
4. Casper (1972) cites the following amusing comment by a defendant:
   Did you have a lawyer when you went to court the next day?
   No. I had a public defender. [p. 101]
5. Somewhat similar views have also been expressed by Sudnow (1965); Skolnick (1967); Casper (1972); Carlen (1976).
6. Some writers have argued that even the radical lawyer may be compromised by such a system, for an unwillingness to engage in informal plea bargaining discussions and a reluctance to foster good relations with others in the system that such discussions invariably necessitate will generally have the effect of penalising clients (see especially Grosman, 1969; Battle, 1971; Oppenheimer, 1973).
7. Cf. Casper (1972) p. 105: 'When a defendant thinks of the public defender as one of "them" rather than as someone on "his" side he is, in an organisational sense, probably right.'
8. See, for instance, D. A. Thomas (1970); Samuels (1971); Hobbs (1971); McConville (1974); Fox and O'Brien (1975). And see *R.* v. *Lester* [1976] Crim.L.R. 389; *R.* v. *Hearne* [1976] Crim.L.R. 753.

9. It is not clear in law what is the precise effect of the guilty plea. In *Riley* (1896) 18 Cox 285, p. 296, Hawkins J. said that the defendant by pleading guilty admits simply that he is guilty of the offence charged in the indictment; he does not thereby admit the truth of the facts stated in the depositions. However, in *Bhagwan* [1970] 1 All E.R. 1129, Widgery L.J. said that by a plea of guilty the defendant admits the facts alleged in the particulars of the indictment. Cf. *Huchison* [1972] 1 All E.R. 936.

10. Useful summaries of the literature on this subject are given in Hills (1971) chs 1 and 2, and Chambliss and Seidman (1971) especially chs 1–5 and 19.

11. *Task Force Report: The Courts*, President's Commission on Law Enforcement and the Administration of Justice, 1967, p. 12. (See also the quote from Chambliss cited above p. 14; Kuh, 1966–7; Bennett, 1976.)

12. For further details of the information supplied by the police in this regard, see above chapter 1, pp. 13–14. Questionnaires were completed by the police on each defendant in the sample and all but two of these were returned.

13. Baldwin and McConville (1974) pp. 440–1. See also Morris (1951); Hammond and Chayen (1963); West (1963); Mack (1976).

14. The police estimates of professionalism tend to be somewhat higher for defendants in this sample of cases than for the very much larger sample of all defendants tried over the same time period in the Birmingham Crown Court.

15. On this, see Avison (1966); McClintock and Avison (1968) ch. 3; Mack (1972); Fordham (1972).

16. What we have aimed to measure, but have done so only in a highly imperfect way, are some of the indices of professionalism as suggested by Sutherland and Cressey (1960) who write: 'The term "professional" when applied to a criminal refers to the following things: the pursuit of crime as a regular, day-by-day occupation, the development of skilled techniques and careful planning in that occupation, and status among criminals.' (p. 232)

17. See particularly Cressey (1972) pp. 44–8; McIntosh (1975) ch. 1.

18. Three of them arrived at the police station in the company of their solicitors, having got wind of the fact that the police were looking for them. In each of these cases, the solicitor was present throughout the interview.

19. To this extent, the results fail to support the hypothesis, developed and tested in the United States by Nagel (1967; 1970), relating to the discrimination experienced by socially disadvantaged groups, such as the lower class, the poor, the uneducated and members of minority groups, when they appear in court. No rigorous test of this hypothesis was possible here since the number of defendants in our sample who were not members of socially disadvantaged groups is in fact very small. Interestingly, however, there was no evidence whatever that this small number of individuals received more favourable treatment than others in the sample, the great majority feeling that they received rough

99

justice in their cases. It may be the case, however, that the system of negotiated justice operates primarily for the socially disadvantaged. Within the narrow confines of the present study, this must remain a matter for conjecture.

6 SOCIAL AND LEGAL IMPLICATIONS

In earlier chapters of this book, we have been primarily concerned with defendants' experiences. Whilst it is necessary, of course, to treat with caution the stories related by these defendants, we do not for our part think it right that they should be dismissed. In this concluding chapter, we shall discuss the more important complaints of defendants, and examine some of the possible remedies for this situation. Though it is necessary to question the behaviour of certain individuals with whom the defendant comes into contact, it is appropriate in our view to regard many of the experiences of defendants not as products of coercive or unethical conduct on the part of these individuals but rather as manifestations of deficiencies in the system as a whole. With this consideration in mind, we shall argue that, unless there is some reassessment of the basic assumptions made about the fair and efficient administration of justice, the inequities of which defendants complained are likely to persist.

If we view the system as a whole, the fate of most defendants is likely to be determined largely by what happens at two specific stages: when he is in the custody of the police following arrest, and when he appears at court for the final hearing. What happens to the defendant at the police station is not unrelated to what happens to him at court. It is the case, for instance, that the nature of the advice given to him by counsel tends to be heavily influenced by the existence of any statement or oral admission made whilst in police custody. But there is another critical consideration that heavily colours what happens to the defendant; this is the pervasive influence of the sentencing discount that is given in return for a guilty plea. It is the events at the police station when the defendant is being questioned and the existence of the discount system that, in our view, explain in large part the way in which the defendant is dealt with by his advisers and by the court, and it is appropriate to deal with these two matters first.

Few people can regard the practice of interrogation of suspects at the police station without a certain unease. At present, police conduct in interrogating suspects is governed by the Judges' Rules, which, as Lord Devlin (1960) said, 'seek to regulate legitimate methods of inquiry'. Broadly the Rules indicate that, although a police officer is entitled to question any person, there is no power to require an answer and a failure to reply does not amount to obstructing a police officer in the execution of his duty.[1] The Rules further provide for the cautioning of suspects at certain points in the interrogation. Accompanying administrative directions lay down, among other things, that reasonable arrangements be made for the comfort and refreshment of persons being questioned, and that, as long as it would not hamper the investigation, a person in custody should be allowed to speak on the telephone to his solicitor or his friends. The Judges' Rules do not have the force of law; the trial judge may, in his discretion, exclude evidence obtained in breach of the Rules. Although their precise meaning is subject to dispute,[2] it now appears that any statement that is voluntary[3] will be admitted in evidence even though obtained in breach of the Rules.[4] More importantly, there can be little doubt that the conduct of police officers during interrogation is frequently at variance with the Judges' Rules, as almost all serving police officers will readily concede. In 1929 the Royal Commission on Police Powers stated:

> We have received a volume of responsible evidence which it is impossible to ignore suggesting that a number of the voluntary statements now tendered in court are not 'voluntary' in the strict sense of the word.

A similar point was made over thirty years later by another

Royal Commission on the police,[5] and some evidence of improper practices has been discussed by other commentators.[6] The results of our own study, to which we have referred in' earlier chapters, convince us that not only are the Judges' Rules frequently broken but that current practices of detention and questioning by the police are such as would be regarded by any fair-minded person as questionable, to say the least. Indeed these practices appear likely to prejudice the guilty and the innocent suspect alike. There is no doubt that in most cases the police are convinced that they have the guilty man before them, though they may well feel that strict compliance with the Judges' Rules is incompatible with effective law enforcement. Equally it is true that there is little incentive for strict adherence to the Rules when it is clear that there is a tendency for the courts to admit evidence obtained in breach of them. Smith (1960) states the dilemma well when he writes:

> If the police need the power to question prisoners, it would be much better if this could be openly stated and some provision made for safeguards against abuse. [p. 349]

Commentators are by and large agreed that the existing safeguards afforded by the Judges' Rules to suspects in police custody are inadequate and various possibilities for strengthening these safeguards have, from time to time, been canvassed. These possibilities include the presence of the suspect's solicitor during questioning,[7] the compulsory examination before a magistrate or a person of similar standing,[8] and the removal of the accused from the custody of the police to the custody of the prison authorities before questioning can take place.[9] More recently, the Criminal Law Revision Committee[10] found themselves divided on the question of what safeguards should surround interrogation at the police station. In general terms, the Committee proposed that where an accused fails to mention during interrogation any fact subsequently relied upon in his defence,[11] the court or jury may draw such inferences as appear proper for the purpose of determining whether to commit for trial, to hold that there

103

is a case to answer, or in deciding whether he is guilty of the offence charged. As a minority of the Committee put it, the practical effect of this recommendation is 'to put a measure of compulsion upon suspects to answer questions, even when they are in custody'.[12] As a consequence of these proposals it was recommended that the content of the Judges' Rules be replaced by new administrative directions by the Home Office and that the present caution be abolished and a written notice be introduced instead, advising the accused to disclose his defence and indicating the dangers if he does not do so. It is against this background that the Committee considered the possibility of introducing safeguards for a suspect at the interrogation stage. The Committee did not favour the suggestion that provision should be made for interrogation of suspects before magistrates on the grounds, *inter alia*, that the formality of the procedure would be likely to inhibit suspects in answering questions, and that it would be difficult to arrange for magistrates to be present when required. One important suggestion, which had been earlier mooted by Williams (1960), that interrogations be tape-recorded, was looked upon by the Committee in a more favourable light. The majority of the Committee were of the view that, although the police in conjunction with the Home Office ought carefully to consider the possibilities of a wider use of tape-recorders and that experiments should be made in order to see how far their use would be helpful, the time was not right to make the use of tape-recorders compulsory.[13]

It now appears that the Committee's proposals regarding the interrogation of suspects have died a speedy and largely unlamented death. This has left the question of police interrogation largely unresolved. Although the Committee's proposals in this respect have been condemned by many critics on the grounds that they represent a fundamental erosion of a defendant's rights,[14] there can be little doubt that the protections afforded to defendants under their proposals would not have represented any deterioration in the present *de facto* situation. It appears to us that, whatever the fate of the Committee's proposals, some additional safeguards ought,

104

as a matter of urgency, to be introduced. The results that have emerged from our study, and that are supported by hundreds of other interviews we have conducted with defendants either acquitted or convicted (carried out as part of our main study of contested trials), lead us to the conclusion that the present position concerning the interrogation of suspects in police custody is highly unsatisfactory. As there is no independent check on what happens to a suspect whilst being questioned by the police, and a deep conviction amongst many serving police officers that the Judges' Rules, if followed, would impede efficient law enforcement, the Rules must not only be consistently violated but many police officers must in consequence be prepared daily to commit perjury by denying that such violations occurred. This fosters a cynical attitude to the law amongst both suspects and police officers, and leaves the suspect (since a police officer's evidence *is* generally preferred to that of the defendant) without any real protection. It seems to us, therefore, that in practice the police station is sometimes a law unto itself, and a law that resorts to dubious practices in order to ensure that what is believed, no doubt in all honesty, to be justice is done. In our view, it is imperative that this situation be remedied.[15]

The importance of the defendant's initial encounter with the police can scarcely be overstated for, in the great majority of cases, what takes place at that stage can critically influence what happens at later stages of the criminal process.[16] Many of the cases we discussed in chapter 4 of possibly innocent men pleading guilty were cases of defendants who said they were persuaded or forced into making statements admitting involvement in the charges alleged. They were very strongly urged by their counsel, no doubt often realistically, not to attempt to contest the matter in court. It appears to us, then, that if adequate checks were to operate at the earliest stage in the criminal process, the defects that in consequence occur at later stages would be considerably reduced.

The second main characteristic of the criminal justice system that underlies, and gives rise to, many of the defects

105

we have described is the practice of awarding a reduction in sentence in return for a guilty plea. Indeed, this customary concession to defendants who indicate their apparent contrition by pleading guilty is fundamental to sentencing in Anglo-American jurisdictions.[17] Yet, despite the fact that this principle is at the very heart of many of the problems we have described throughout this book, it remains the case that the question of a sentencing discount being offered to defendants who plead guilty has been raised relatively infrequently by commentators.[18] There is a widespread belief that to question the discount principle is to indulge in rather fanciful speculation for, it is argued, the administration of justice would rapidly become overwhelmed by contested cases if it were no longer to operate. Glanville Williams has described the system as 'an unhappy necessity' and he summarises concisely the arguments in favour of it as follows:

> ... offenders who have no defence must be persuaded not to waste the time of the court and public money; pleas of guilty often save the distress of witnesses in having to give evidence, as well as inconvenience and loss of time; and in present conditions such pleas are essential to prevent serious congestion in the courts.[19]

There can be no doubting the administrative expediency of the discount principle, and there would be without question a considerable increase in the number of contested trials if it did not operate.[20] It may seem, then, in this light, unrealistic to argue for the abolition of the principle, or even for a reassessment of the premises upon which it is based. Certainly current thinking in England is strongly against us in this regard and official policy is directed at seeking ways of reducing the number of cases that go for trial in the Crown Court rather than increasing it.[21] Yet the injustices that we have ourselves seen at first hand compel us to draw attention to the potentially coercive element that permeates the judicial process brought about by the existence of the discount principle. The problem is quite simply that it may induce

106

the innocent to plead guilty as well as the guilty. Further-more, the greater the disparities, or, more accurately, the anticipated disparities, between sentences following a guilty and a not guilty plea, the greater the risk that innocent defendants will plead guilty. On the evidence of our research, we would argue that the mere existence of the principle lends legitimacy to unfair pressures exerted on defendants by lawyers and may even be seen to justify them.

The legal justification for the discount as it applies in England is often lost on defendants. As a rule, they see it operating to penalise those who decide to contest their cases rather than, as the courts see it, as a mitigating factor in sentencing those who demonstrate their remorse by pleading guilty. D. A. Thomas (1970), in his analysis of Appeal Court decisions, states the principle in the following way:

> The court has frequently stated that while in an appropriate case the offender's remorse in pleading guilty may be treated as a mitigating factor, his insistence on being tried can never justify an aggravation of his sentence beyond the ceiling justified by the facts of the offence ... The same principle applies to cases where the offender makes allegations against police or other prosecution witnesses, or appears to commit perjury in the course of his defence. Such behaviour does not justify any increase in his sentence above what is appropriate for the offence, but the offender may lose some credit which might otherwise go to mitigate his sentence. [pp. 52–3]

There is a curious logic in this, and it is very easy to understand why defendants regard this reasoning as hollow and meaningless. Nor are defendants alone in thinking this. Although it is sometimes asserted that the discount in favour of the accused who pleads guilty will be given only where there is actual evidence of remorse and repentance,[22] courts do not customarily make enquiries of the defendant on these matters and often appear to content themselves with the view that the guilty plea is in itself indicative of remorse. It emerged from the interviews that we conducted that defendants were given the distinct impression by their counsel

107

that such a reduction was in fact automatic. Furthermore, it was abundantly clear from the interviews that expressions of genuine remorse were exceedingly rare. Indeed, the mere fact that over half of the defendants in the sample were still protesting their innocence, in some cases weeks after the sentence had been passed, is evidence of this. No more than half a dozen defendants could be said to be contrite; indeed, expressions of cynicism, bitterness and anger are much commoner than remorse or contrition.[23]

The crux of the argument in favour of the discount principle is, as we see it, that defendants must be strongly discouraged from wasting the valuable time of the court by needlessly fighting lost causes. It is assumed in this that lawyers can readily identify those cases that are hopeless and can therefore advise their clients of the risks of fighting the case in court. It seems to us that there are great dangers in this assumption. The results we have presented in chapter 4 of this book suggest that there may well be considerable disagreement, even amongst experts, about whether a particular case is hopeless or not. If we are to accept the validity of the results we have presented in chapter 4 relating to the predictions of our independent assessors, then we are forced to conclude that while some counsel *are* able to identify the hopeless case, others can do so only in a highly imprecise way. The dangers to an innocent man in this situation require no further elaboration.

We remain unconvinced that, even if a defendant deliberately wastes the court's time, what amounts to an accretion to his sentence of the order of a quarter to a third is thereby justified. It is customary to boast of a man's fundamental right to ask the prosecution to prove their case beyond reasonable doubt, yet the man is penalised when the prosecution is able to do so. Either it is a right or it is not, and we regard the present confusion and ambiguity surrounding it as indicative of the hypocrisy that tends often to characterise discussions on this subject. Professor Gordon Trasler has called into question this issue of wasting the courts' time and writes:

Counsel and judges ... may ... complain of the waste of their time. Yet their time (unlike that of the accused, should he be convicted) is sufficiently repaid in guineas; the cost falls not upon them, but upon the people at large, who may be content to pay a price for the assurance that others will not be convicted upon inadequate evidence ... [T]o impose so severe a penalty for wasting the time of a group of notably well-paid men seems excessive.[24]

The operation of the discount system has in our view little to do with justice; it exists primarily because of administrative expediency.[25] There may well be truth in the assertion that without it courts would rapidly become submerged by the volume of cases with which they would have to deal. It must be remembered, however, that many cases that currently end in a late guilty plea would, on the evidence we have put forward, be fit and proper cases for jury trial.[26]

It is against this background of tension at either end of the legal process that the conduct of counsel and of the court must be examined. Throughout this book we have drawn attention to the strong pressures brought to bear by certain barristers in order to induce defendants to plead guilty. We should re-emphasise the point made in chapter 3 that in a majority of cases within this sample the conduct of counsel was not seriously criticised by defendants. The question nonetheless remains: why was it that a third of barristers in the sample were seen by defendants as behaving in an oppressive or dismissive way? Unfortunately, we can only speculate about the reasons for this situation,[27] but we do not believe, as is clear from chapter 4, that the strength of the prosecution case alone is a sufficient explanation in more than a minority of cases. We had anticipated that those cases in which defendants said they had pleaded guilty in response to pressure from their barrister would be mainly cases in which the defendant had originally made a statement to the police and cases that many barristers would, in consequence, regard to all intents and purposes as hopeless. Yet only slightly more than a third of all defendants within this group had made statements to the police, and some of these statements were admissions to only some of the counts to which the defendant subsequently pleaded guilty and a few did not amount to admissions at all. It is important to note that, of defendants who said they had pleaded guilty in response to pressure from defence counsel, a lower proportion had made statements to the police than for the sample as a whole. The following table, which is based on the categories described in chapter 2, sets out the proportions:

Reason given by defendant for pleading guilty	No. of defendants	% making statements to the police
Defendant guilty as pleaded	35	51.4
Plea bargain	22	45.5
Tacit plea bargain	16	43.8
Pressure from barrister	48	35.4
	121	43.0

Other factors than the strength of the prosecution case must be at work. One is the pressure of work on barristers in Birmingham. The demands of the court and of their practice in general are such that few barristers can be sure, even if the brief is delivered in good time, that they will be available to conduct a particular defence. Counsel may, therefore, be understandably reluctant to spend an undue amount of time on a case, digesting the evidence, giving advice and preparing for trial, if there is a likelihood that on the day it is listed for trial he is part-heard in another case or for one reason or another not going to be available. The result is, as many solicitors have told us, that some barristers are often not sufficiently familiar with the brief properly to advise the defendant. In consequence, they may on occasion undertake a course that, with the benefit of more careful thought, may be ill-considered. How barristers respond to these pressures is, of course, very much a matter of individual experience and temperament. Another difficulty is that the barrister who ultimately undertakes the defence is quite often not the person initially selected. In such cases, the brief is commonly returned so late that it is almost impossible for a barrister to give the case adequate consideration.[28] Because of lack of preparation, it is possible that some barristers may be reluctant to undertake the defence of a case in court. For some cases this would appear to be a reasonable explanation and, for other cases, it was certainly the impression that was given by the barrister concerned to the defendant.

It is also arguable that counsel's primary interests inevitably lie with the court system and not with the defendant. We have already discussed in chapter 5 the pressures that the court organisation itself imposes on those who work within it. There is often great pressure upon counsel to deliver what the system wants, and one of the over-riding requirements is, as we see it, administrative efficiency, which is greatly assisted by—indeed in large part dependent upon—a steady flow of guilty pleas. The discount system is itself one manifestation of this concern. It may well benefit counsel, who may be briefed for the prosecution on the next case, to work within the administrative goals of the system, to ensure a steady flow of cases.[29] In some cases, the immediate pressures on barristers themselves to deliver a plea may be considerable. Take for example the sort of case commonly commented upon by solicitors where the trial judge has spoken to both counsel and expressed the view he has formed of the case on the basis of the committal documents in his possession. It may well be that, if the judge expresses a strong opinion, defence counsel (particularly if young and inexperienced) may feel inhibited in the sort of advice he can give to a defendant and reluctant to embark upon a course that would be contrary to the judge's expressed view.

Turning for the moment to the prosecution side, it is important to discuss one factor that many observers in the United States see as the dominant factor behind the induced guilty plea. This is the practice in those courts of deliberately 'over-charging' defendants in order to pressure them into pleading guilty to a lesser count. Thus, for example, a man who has committed an indecent assault might be charged with the more serious count of rape, not with a view to gaining a conviction on the rape charge but simply to induce the defendant to plead guilty to indecent assault. Many writers on plea bargaining regard this kind of over-charging of defendants as standard practice in many jurisdictions in the United States,[30] though observers have found little evidence of it in England. McCabe and Purves (1972a), for instance, found that though the prosecution commonly charged fully (in the sense that they inserted 'every charge which could reasonably be said to arise from the situation even when it is clear that it is unlikely that every charge could be proved on the evidence available') they could find no evidence of over-charging.

We were able to examine the question of over-charging of suspects in somewhat greater detail than McCabe and Purves could. As outlined in earlier chapters, we had the committal papers relating to each case in the sample examined rigorously and independently by two experienced assessors who attempted on the basis of that evidence to predict the likely outcome of the cases. No fewer than 84 per cent of defendants faced indictments containing at least two counts,[31] and a third faced indictments with four or more. These figures might suggest that some over-charging of defendants could have occurred. This turned out, however, to be largely unsupported by the views of the assessors. We examined the predictions they made according to their views of the likely outcome of the principal count in the indictment. If there had been systematic over-charging of defendants in Birmingham, we would have anticipated that the assessors would have identified the principal count as a likely acquittal. Yet in only a quarter of all cases did one of the assessors anticipate an acquittal on the principal count, and in only slightly more than one in ten cases did both assessors predict this. Insofar as this measure provides any indication, there is then no real evidence to suggest systematic over-charging of defendants in Birmingham in order to prompt a guilty plea.[32]

We have described in chapter 5 how defendants are often aggrieved because they feel that, once they have pleaded guilty in court, the matter is, as it were, taken out of their hands and they are then powerless to affect the course of events. A consequence of this is that many of them complain that it is the prosecution's version of events that is accepted by the court (and that may in large part determine the sentence) even though it is, in their view, frequently incomplete or distorted. All such distortion before the court produces a sense of injustice, and the question arises whether anything can be done to eliminate it. Such checks as exist appear to be largely ineffective and the courts have generally failed to develop other than rudimentary procedures for ensuring that an accurate version of the offence is presented in cases involving a guilty plea. Although the judge may enquire into any matter in respect of which he requires information and may request the prosecution to elaborate any aspect of the facts of a case,[33] it appears that this is rarely done in practice. In plain terms, surprisingly little care is taken in probing into cases where there is a guilty plea. One important consequence of this is that, during the course of the hearing, awkward or potentially embarrassing questions concerning, say, the conduct of investigating police officers or of lawyers involved in the case, are only exceptionally raised. Though we do not suggest here any 'conspiracy of silence' amongst the incumbents of the legal system, there is at the same time no doubting the advantages of the superficial nature of the enquiry undertaken by the court in such cases. Disquieting aspects of many of the cases we examined, which the defendants concerned wanted aired in court, remained hidden.[34] The guilty pleas in these cases are so intimately related to the sentencing functions of the court that the fullest possible information should be available to the judge before sentence is passed. It is not, however, easy to see how such information could be obtained. In the United States, in federal courts and in some state courts, there is a requirement that the judge ascertain that there is a factual basis for the plea and also that the plea is not entered in breach of 'due process' requirements. But most commentators are agreed that questioning of the accused by the judge in the United States about these matters

113

represents a largely meaningless ritual in which the defendant assures the court that no bargain has been struck and that no pressure has been brought to bear when everyone present knows that this is manifestly not the case.[35] The reason for the ineffectiveness of such procedures is not hard to find. At the stage when these apparent safeguards are introduced, the defendant is already a consenting party to the court-room charade because he has been led to believe, as is indeed often the case, that a guilty plea is his best or only course of action; he has in effect been co-opted into a system that places more importance on empty ceremony than on the strict observance of due process of law. That the courts in England do not engage in this form of empty ritual is not necessarily to be applauded; rather, it is evidence of the failure of the English court system to identify a fundamental weakness in the guilty plea procedure. One possible solution to these difficulties might be to improve these procedures, and a number of proposals have been made to this end by several writers.[36] Two of these proposals might be mentioned here. In the first place, it might be possible for the prosecution, in cases in which a guilty plea is likely, to provide the defendant and his counsel in advance of trial with a statement of the facts on which they intend to rely in court. This would give notice to the defendant of one of the consequences of a guilty plea and would perhaps provide an opportunity of settling any disputed matter before the hearing. Second, the courts could develop fixed procedures for settling disputed facts relating to the commission of the offence or to sentence, and the judge could be required to give reasons for his determination on disputed issues.

These modifications to existing procedures would, however, provide no more than a partial answer, for what appears to be lacking is the will to enforce any safeguards. For example, the courts have laid down a set of rules, analogous to the Judges' Rules, which attempt to set acceptable limits within which advice may be given to the accused by his legal advisers. The *Turner* case in particular has been seen by many writers as setting strict controls on the growth of plea bargaining practices. In our view, these provisions are too imprecise adequately to ensure either that an accused is given proper advice or that a plea of guilty resulting from pre-trial discussions with counsel is voluntary. But it seems unlikely that any re-formulation of these rules by judges would greatly strengthen the protection of the accused.

We suggested at the beginning of this chapter that the defects in the practice of negotiated guilty pleas we have discussed in this book are not primarily explicable in terms of misguided conduct on the part of lawyers, police officers or others but more fundamentally in terms of deficiencies in the criminal justice system. Indeed, we see the irregular behaviour of those within the system principally as accommodations to two basic factors—the interrogation of suspects whilst in police custody and the practice of allowing a discount in sentence where there is a plea of guilty. We are firmly of the view that, notwithstanding the introduction of rules to control the advice of counsel or modifications to court-room procedures, it is only if these two matters are remedied that the injustices we have described can be eliminated.

In the course of our enquiries we became very conscious of the difficulties that confront police officers, practitioners, court officials and others, and of the problems posed for them by a system that is chronically under-financed and overburdened. That we have not given more space to a consideration of these problems is not because we do not sympathise with those who are forced to operate within these constraints; rather it is because in our view these aspects of the situation are of secondary importance compared with the problems of injustice we have encountered in the course of our research. Though lack of resources inevitably creates pressures at all stages of the criminal process to minimise the number of cases tried by jury, the problems of injustice that we have described are not attributable merely to lack of finance. The injustices we have encountered are, in our judgment, essentially the product of a system that gives too little protection to the innocent and too often sacrifices the needs of the individual to the requirements of bureaucratic efficiency. This in turn manifests

115

itself in the adoption of standards of behaviour that, though they may well make sense within a system of values thus warped, are often seen by defendants as oppressive. We should at least be aware that, if we continue to pay scant regard to the rights of suspects and to devote insufficient resources to the administration of justice, we are perpetuating a system of negotiated justice that, with some frequency, produces results of a fundamentally inequitable nature.

NOTES AND REFERENCES

1. *Rice* v. *Connolly* [1966] 2 Q.B. 414.
2. See, for instance, Brownlie (1967); Thompson (1967).
3. A statement is not 'voluntary' if it was made in consequence of an improper inducement or threat of a temporal nature held out or made by a person in authority, or by oppression. See Cross, *Evidence* (1974) pp. 482 ff.
4. See *Praeger* [1972] 1 All E.R. 1114.
5. Cmnd. 1728, 1962, para. 369.
6. See, for example, Williams (1960) pp. 328–31; Zander (1972a).
7. Williams (1960) p. 344. Lord Widgery C.J. has been quoted as saying that such a rule is 'quite unacceptable', *The Times*, 17 July 1971.
8. Justice Reports (1967, 1972); Williams (1960) p. 345.
9. Williams (1960) pp. 345–6. This proposal is criticised by Smith (1960, p. 352) on the grounds that there would be insufficient protection against malpractices other than violence.
10. *Evidence (General)*, *11th Report*, 1972, Cmnd. 4991.
11. And being one which he could 'reasonably have been expected to mention' in all the circumstances (paras 32 and 35).
12. Para. 52(iv).
13. A minority of three members of the Committee went further and recommended that statutory provision be made for the compulsory use of tape-recorders at police stations in the larger centres of population and that the Committee's proposal regarding adverse inferences from silence under police questioning should not be implemented until this had been done (see para. 52). See, generally, Ashworth (1976).
14. The most important criticisms have been raised by the General Council of the Bar (1973); the National Council for Civil Liberties (1973); and the Release Lawyers' Group (1973). See also the balanced discussion of the 'right to silence' in Greenawalt (1974).
15. A Home Office Steering Committee formed in April 1975 to consider the feasibility of an experiment in the tape-recording of police interrogations reported in October 1976. Without commenting on the desirability of such an experiment, the Committee were of the view that a limited experiment would be feasible. According to newspaper reports, the Police

Federation has expressed its total opposition to even this limited experiment (*The Times*, 20 October 1976). Whilst we are aware of the many practical problems posed by the use of tape-recorders during interrogation, it seems to us unlikely that such problems are greater than the manifest injustices caused by the present unregulated system.

16. On this point, see chapter 5 above and the discussion in Bottoms and McClean (1976) p. 230.
17. See, for instance, D. A. Thomas (1970) ch. 2.
18. Even the empirical studies conducted by criminologists concerned with the question of sentencing disparities have tended to pay scant attention to the complex, though crucial, variable of the defendant's plea. (On this, see the reviews in Hood and Sparks, 1970, ch. 5 and Bottomley, 1973, pp. 133–55.) One important exception to this is the study by Green (1961).
19. See his letter to *The Times*, 25 February 1976. This letter provoked a lively correspondence in the newspaper for several days.
20. There have been marked differences of view as to the extent of this increase. On this, see particularly, Folberg (1968); McIntyre and Lippman (1970); Ferguson and Roberts (1974); Finkelstein (1975); Heumann (1975); Bayley (1976).
21. On this, see the Report of the Interdepartmental Committee (Chairman Lord Justice James) *The Distribution of Criminal Business between the Crown Court and the Magistrates' Court* (1975) Cmnd. 6323.
22. See, for instance, Davis (1971) particularly pp. 152–3. Cf. Paul Thomas (1970).
23. Our results correspond with the conclusion of Rosett (1967) who states with characteristic bluntness: 'One may doubt whether many of the defendants who "cop a plea" on any given day are motivated by this sort of spiritual awakening. In many courts, the guilty-plea process looks more like the purchase of a rug in a Lebanese bazaar than like the confrontation between a man and his soul.' (p. 75)
24. In a letter to *The Times* (28 February 1976). See also the classic demolition of other arguments buttressing the discount principle in the comment in the *Yale Law Journal* (1956) p. 204; also in the Note in the *University of Chicago Law Review* (1964) and the Note in *Harvard Law Review* (1977).
25. The actual saving of time, money and scarce resources caused by late changes of plea appears, however, to be limited; see Purves (1971) pp. 473–4.
26. As noted in chapter 1, the proportion of defendants who plead guilty in the Birmingham Crown Court is higher than for any other Crown Court centre for which statistics are available.
27. These speculations are based in large part on discussions we have had with solicitors, barristers and court officers.
28. See also McCabe and Purves (1972a) who write:
    . . . last minute changes of plea involve conferences convened quickly and discussions conducted in haste. It might well be asked whether briefs should not be delivered and conferences held at an earlier stage, and whether barristers should be less ready to dispose of briefs to their colleagues at so late a stage that the counsel into whose hands the

brief ultimately falls has only the shortest familiarity with its contents. [p. 44]

The following comment of Danks (1975), Chief Prosecuting Solicitor in Hampshire, gives some idea of the scope of the problem:

> The problem of the returned brief is not only a difficulty for barristers but also for solicitors. One day I had 25 briefs returned, one afternoon, seven of them fights, and all of them for the next day. This is no way to run a business and it ought not to be beyond the wit of the legal profession to design a system which avoids such difficulties, or at least alleviates the position. [pp. 70–1]

29. The common pool of barristers is in this sense not a mark of the independence of the profession; rather it might be seen to facilitate what one writer has called 'a delicate mutual back-scratching system' (see Parker, 1971).

30. See, for example, President's Commission, *Task Force Report* (1967); Folberg (1968); *Harvard Law Review* (1970); Downie (1971); *Yale Law Journal* (1972); and Parker (1972).

31. 26 per cent of defendants, however, faced indictments with two counts that were direct alternatives. Hence 58 per cent of indictments included at least two substantive counts; cf. McCabe and Purves (1972a) where the corresponding figure is 39.2 per cent.

32. The results provide some evidence that individual defendants were overcharged but these cases are relatively rare. This supports the view that was expressed to us quite unequivocally by the Chief Prosecuting Solicitor of the West Midlands. He stated:

> The purpose of an indictment, as I understand it, is accurately to present to the court in indictment or charge form the offences that are disclosed on the prosecution evidence. To put additional counts into the indictment purely and simply as an exercise to try and force a defendant to plead to the matter you really have in mind is, in my view, improper [interviewed September 1976].

33. *Van Pelz* [1943] K.B. 157; *Hearne* [1976] Crim.L.R. 753.

34. There is a voluminous literature on this aspect of the guilty plea process. See, for example, Alschuler (1968); Blumberg (1970b); Laurie (1972) especially pp. 215–19; Heberling (1973); Newman (1973); Wishingrad (1974); Goldstein (1975); Gilboy (1976).

35. See, for instance, White (1971); Chambliss and Seidman (1971); Katz, Litwin and Bamberger (1972); Note, *Catholic Law* (1975).

36. See D. A. Thomas (1970); Samuels (1971).

CASES

[Cases are listed under the name of the accused whenever the usual method of citation would cause them to be preceded by the abbreviation '*R. v.*' signifying that the prosecution was undertaken by the Crown.]

Alexander (1912) 7 Cr.App.R. 110
Ali Tasamulug [1971] Crim.L.R. 441
Baker (1912) 28 T.L.R. 363
Bhagwan [1970] 1 All E.R. 1129
Cain [1976] Crim.L.R. 464
Chadwicke, The Times, 22 November 1932
Claxton [1965] Crim.L.R. 737
Coe (1969) 53 Cr.App.R. 66
Dunbar (1966) 51 Cr.App.R. 57
Ellis (1973) 57 Cr.App.R. 571
Golathan (1915) 84 L.J.K.B. 758
Griffiths (1932) 23 Cr.App.R. 153
Hall (1968) 52 Cr.App.R. 528
Hearne [1976] Crim.L.R. 753
Heyes [1951] 1 K.B. 29
Huchison [1972] 1 All E.R. 936
Ingleson [1915] 1 K.B. 512
Kelly [1961] Crim.L.R. 564
Lester [1976] Crim.L.R. 389
Lloyd (1923) 17 Cr.App.R. 184
O'Leary [1965] Crim.L.R. 56
People, The v. *Castro*, 356 N.Y.S. 2d 49 (1974)
People, The v. *Foster*, 225 N.E. 2d 200 (N.Y. 1967)
People, The v. *Morris*, 289 N.E. 2d 635 (1972)
People, The v. *Williams*, 354 N.Y.S. 2d 213 (1974)

Plimmer [1975] Crim.L.R. 730

Praeger [1972] 1 All E.R. 1114

Quartey [1975] Crim.L.R. 592

Regan [1959] Crim.L.R. 529

Rice v. *Connolly* [1966] 2 Q.B. 414

Riley (1896) 18 Cox 285

Soanes (1948) 32 Cr.App.R. 136

Thomas and Whittle, Unreported 28.4.67, 741/67

Turner (1970) 54 Cr.App.R. 352

U.S. v. *Birmingham*, 454 F.2d 706 (10th Cir. 1971)

U.S. v. *Rushing*, 456 F.2d 1294 (5th Cir. 1972)

Van Pelz [1943] K.B. 157

Waddy v. *Heer*, 383 F.2d 789 (6th Cir. 1967)

BIBLIOGRAPHY

A.B.A. Standards for Criminal Justice Relating to Pleas of Guilty American Bar Association (1968).

J. E. Adams 'The Second Ethical Problem in R. v. Turner; The Limits of an Advocate's Discretion' *Criminal Law Review* (1971) pp. 252–64.

A. W. Alschuler 'The Prosecutor's Role in Plea Bargaining' *University of Chicago Law Review* Vol. 36 (1968) pp. 50–112.

A. W. Alschuler 'Defence Attorney's Role in Plea Bargaining' *Yale Law Journal* Vol. 84 (1975) pp. 1179–314.

Annual Survey of American Law (1966) 'Plea Bargaining' pp. 537–52.

A. F. Arcuri 'Lawyers, Judges, and Plea Bargaining: Some New Data on Inmates' Views' *International Journal of Criminology and Penology* Vol. 4 (1976) pp. 177–91.

F. V. Ariano and J. W. Countryman 'The Role of Plea Negotiation in Modern Criminal Law' *Chicago–Kent Law Review* Vol. 46 (1969) pp. 116–122.

A. J. Ashworth 'Some Blueprints for Criminal Investigation' *Criminal Law Review* (1976) pp. 594–609.

N. Avison 'The New Pattern of Crime' *New Society* (8 September 1966) pp. 358–60.

J. Baldwin and M. J. McConville 'The Acquittal Rate of Professional Criminals: A Critical Note' *Modern Law Review* Vol. 37 (1974) pp. 439–43.

Z. Bankowski and G. Mungham *Images of Law* Routledge and Kegan Paul (1976).

J. B. Battle 'In Search of the Adversary System—The Cooperative Practices of Private Defence Attorneys' *Texas Law Review* Vol. 50 (1971) pp. 60–118.

C. T. Bayley 'Plea Bargaining: An Offer a Prosecutor Can Refuse' *Judicature* Vol. 60 (1976) pp. 229–32.

L. A. Bennett 'An Offer You Can't Refuse: The Current Status of Plea Bargaining in California' *Pacific Law Journal* Vol. 7 (1976) pp. 80–104.

A. S. Blumberg 'The Practice of Law as a Confidence Game: Organizational Co-optation of a Profession' *Law and Society Review* Vol. 1 (1967) pp. 15–39.

A. S. Blumberg (ed.) *The Scales of Justice* Transaction Books (1970a).

A. S. Blumberg *Criminal Justice* Quadrangle Books (1970b).

A. K. Bottomley *Decisions in the Penal Process* Martin Robertson (1973).

A. E. Bottoms and J. D. McClean *Defendants in the Criminal Process* Routledge and Kegan Paul (1976).

121

Sir William Boulton *Conduct and Etiquette at the Bar* 6th edn, Butterworths (1975).

R. Brandon and C. Davies *Wrongful Imprisonment: Mistaken Convictions and their Consequences* Allen and Unwin (1973).

I. Brownlie 'Police Powers—IV' *Criminal Law Review* (1967) pp. 75–91.

P. Carlen *Magistrates' Justice* Martin Robertson (1976).

J. D. Casper *American Criminal Justice: The Defendant's Perspective* Prentice Hall (1972).

Catholic Law, Note 'People v. Selikoff—The Route to Rational Plea Bargaining' *Catholic Law* Vol. 21 (1975) pp. 144–61.

W. J. Chambliss (ed.) *Crime and the Legal Process* McGraw-Hill (1969).

W. J. Chambliss and R. D. Seidman *Law, Order, and Power* Addison-Wesley (1971).

N. Christie 'Conflicts as Property' *British Journal of Criminology* Vol. 17 (1977) pp. 1–15.

H. H. A. Cooper 'Plea-Bargaining: A Comparative Analysis' *New York University Journal of International Law and Politics* Vol. 5 (1972) pp. 427–48.

D. R. Cressey *Criminal Organisation* Heinemann (1972).

Criminal Law Revision Committee *Felonies and Misdemeanours 7th Report* (1965) Cmnd. 2659.

Criminal Law Revision Committee *Evidence (General) 11th Report* (1972) Cmnd. 4991.

R. Cross *Evidence* 4th ed., Butterworths (1974).

P. K. L. Danks 'The Prosecuting Solicitor' pp. 64–73 in 'The Prosecution Process' Proceedings of a Conference held at the University of Birmingham (April 1975).

S. Dash 'Cracks in the Foundation of Criminal Justice' *Illinois Law Review* Vol. 46 (1951) pp. 385–406.

C. Davies 'The Innocent who Plead Guilty' *Law Guardian* (March 1970) pp. 9–15.

A. Davis 'Sentences for Sale: A New Look at Plea Bargaining in England and America' *Criminal Law Review* (1971) pp. 150–61, 218–28.

J. M. Dean 'Illegitimacy of Plea Bargaining' *Federal Probation* Vol. 38 (1974) pp. 18–38.

S. Dell *Silent in Court* Bell (1971).

Lord Devlin *The Criminal Prosecution in England* Oxford University Press (1960).

L. Downie *Justice Denied* Praeger (1971).

A. Enker 'Perspectives on Plea Bargaining' Appendix A in President's Commission on Law Enforcement and Administration of Justice, *Task Force Report: The Courts* Washington, D.C., U.S. Government Printing Office (1967).

E. D. Fay 'The "Bargained for" Guilty Plea' *Criminal Law Bulletin* Vol. 4 (1968) pp. 265–72.

G. A. Ferguson and D. W. Roberts 'Plea Bargaining: Directions for Canadian Reform' *Canadian Bar Review* Vol. 52 (1974) pp. 497–576.

M. O. Finkelstein 'A Statistical Analysis of Guilty Plea Practices in the Federal Courts' *Harvard Law Review* Vol. 89 (1975) pp. 293–315.

H. J. Folberg 'The "Bargained for" Guilty Plea—An Evaluation' *Criminal Law Bulletin* Vol. 4 (1968) pp. 201–12.

P. Fordham *Inside the Underworld* Allen and Unwin (1972).

R. G. Fox and B. M. O'Brien 'Fact-Finding for Sentencers' *Melbourne University Law Review* Vol. 10 (1975) pp. 163–206.

K. Gallagher 'Judicial Participation in Plea Bargaining: A Search for New Standards' *Harvard Civil Rights—Civil Liberties Law Review* Vol. 9 (1974) pp. 29–51.

General Council of the Bar *Evidence in Criminal Cases: Memorandum on the 11th Report of the Criminal Law Revision Committee: Evidence (General)* (1973).

Georgia Law Review 'Criminal Law—Plea Bargaining—Direct Participation by Trial Judge in Plea Bargaining does not Vitiate Voluntariness of Subsequent Guilty Plea' *Georgia Law Review* Vol. 5 (1971) pp. 809–16.

J. A. Gilboy 'Guilty Plea Negotiations and the Exclusionary Rule of Evidence: A Case Study of Chicago Narcotics Courts' *Journal of Criminal Law and Criminology* Vol. 67 (1976) pp. 89–98.

J. Goldstein 'For Harold Lasswell: Some Reflections on Human Dignity, Entrapment, Informed Consent, and the Plea Bargain' *Yale Law Journal* Vol. 84 (1975) pp. 683–703.

E. Green *Judicial Attitudes in Sentencing* Macmillan (1961).

K. Greenawalt 'Perspectives on the Right to Silence' pp. 235–68 in R. Hood (ed.) *Crime, Criminology and Public Policy* Heinemann (1974).

B. A. Grosman *The Prosecutor: An Inquiry into the Exercise of Discretion* University of Toronto Press (1969).

W. H. Hammond and E. Chayen *Persistent Criminals* H.M.S.O. (1963).

Harvard Law Review, Note 'Unconstitutionality of Plea Bargaining' *Harvard Law Review* Vol. 83 (1970) pp. 1387–411.

Harvard Law Review, Note 'Plea Bargaining and the Transformation of the Criminal Process' *Harvard Law Review* Vol. 90 (1977) pp. 564–95.

J. L. Heberling 'Conviction Without Trial' *Anglo-American Law Review* Vol. 2 (1973) pp. 428–72.

M. Heumann 'A Note on Plea Bargaining and Case Pressure' *Law and Society Review* Vol. 9 (1975) pp. 514–28.

S. L. Hills *Crime, Power, and Morality* Chandler Publishing Company (1971).

G. J. Hobbs 'Judicial Supervision over California Plea Bargaining: Regulating the Trade' *California Law Review* Vol. 59 (1971) pp. 962–96.

Home Office Steering Committee *The Feasibility of an Experiment in the Tape-recording of Police Interrogations* Cmnd. 6630 (1976).

R. Hood and R. Sparks *Key Issues in Criminology* World University Library (1970).

Interdepartmental Committee *The Distribution of Criminal Business between the Crown Court and the Magistrates' Court* (Chairman Lord Justice James) Cmnd. 6323 (1975).

R. M. Jackson *The Machinery of Justice in England* 6th edn, Cambridge University Press (1972).

Justice Report *The Interrogation of Suspects* (1967).

Justice Report *Memorandum on Eleventh Report of the Criminal Law Revision Committee* (1972).

123

H. Kalven and H. Zeisel *The American Jury* University of Chicago Press (1966).

L. R. Katz, L. B. Litwin and R. H. Bamberger *Justice is the Crime: Pretrial Delay in Felony Cases* Cleveland, The Press of Case Western Reserve University (1972).

A. D. Klein 'Plea Bargaining' *Criminal Law Quarterly* Vol. 14 (1972) pp. 289–305.

J. M. Kress 'The Agnew Case: Policy, Prosecution and Plea Bargaining' *Criminal Law Bulletin* Vol. 10 (1974) pp. 80–4.

R. H. Kuh 'Plea Copping' *New York County Bar Bulletin* Vol. 24 (1966–7) pp. 160–7.

W. R. La Fave 'The Prosecutor's Discretion in the United States' *The American Journal of Comparative Law* Vol. 18 (1970) pp. 532–48.

P. Laurie *Scotland Yard* Penguin (1972).

S. McCabe and R. Purves *By-Passing the Jury* Oxford University Penal Research Unit: Blackwell (1972a).

S. McCabe and R. Purves *The Jury at Work* Oxford University Penal Research Unit: Blackwell (1972b).

F. H. McClintock and N. H. Avison *Crime in England and Wales* Heinemann (1968).

M. J. McConville 'Sentencing Issues: Judge and Jury' *University of Western Australia Law Review* Vol. 11 (1974) pp. 230–44.

M. McIntosh *The Organisation of Crime* Macmillan Press (1975).

D. M. McIntyre and D. Lippman 'Prosecutors and Early Dispositions of Felony Cases' *A.B.A. Journal* Vol. 56 (1970) pp. 1154–9.

J. A. Mack 'The Able Criminal' *British Journal of Criminology* Vol. 12 (1972) pp. 44–54.

J. A. Mack 'Full-Time Major Criminals and the Courts' *Modern Law Review* Vol. 39 (1976) pp. 241–67.

Sir Robert Mark *Minority Verdict*, The 1973 Dimbleby Lecture, B.B.C. Publications (1973).

J. P. Martin and D. Webster *Social Consequences of Conviction* Heinemann (1971).

D. Miller 'The Compromise of Criminal Cases' *Southern California Law Review* Vol. 1 (1927) pp. 1–31.

R. Moley 'The Vanishing Jury' *Southern California Law Review* Vol. 2 (1928) pp. 97–127.

N. Morris *The Habitual Criminal* Longmans (1951).

S. S. Nagel 'Disparities in Criminal Procedure' *U.C.L.A. Law Review* Vol. 14 (1967) pp. 1272–1305.

S. S. Nagel 'The Tipped Scales of American Justice' pp. 31–49 in A. S. Blumberg (ed.) *The Scales of Justice* Transaction Books (1970).

National Council for Civil Liberties *The Rights of Suspects* N.C.C.L. (1973).

D. J. Newman 'Pleading Guilty for Considerations: A Study of Bargain Justice' *Journal of Criminal Law, Criminology, and Police Science* Vol. 46 (1956) pp. 780–90.

D. J. Newman *Conviction: the Determination of Guilt or Innocence Without Trial* Boston, Little, Brown (1966).

124

D. J. Newman 'Reshape the Deal' *Trial Magazine* (1973) pp. 11–15.

D. J. Newman and E. C. NeMoyer 'Issues of Propriety in Negotiated Justice' *Denver Law Journal* Vol. 47 (1970) pp. 367–407.

A. N. Oppenheim *Questionnaire Design and Attitude Measurement* Heinemann (1966).

C. Oppenheimer 'Rebel With a Cause: The Movement Lawyer in the Criminal Courts' *American Journal of Criminal Law* Vol. 2 (1973) pp. 146–86.

G. Parker 'Copping a Plea' *Justice of the Peace and Local Government Review* Vol. 135 (1971) pp. 408–9.

J. F. Parker 'Plea Bargaining' *American Journal of Criminal Law* Vol. 2 (1972) pp. 187–209.

President's Commission on Law Enforcement and the Administration of Justice *Task Force Report: The Courts* Washington D.C., U.S. Government Printing Office (1967).

R. Purves 'That Plea Bargaining Business: Some Conclusions from Research' *Criminal Law Review* (1971) pp. 470–5.

Release Lawyers' Group *Guilty Until Proved Innocent* (1973).

A. Rosett 'The Negotiated Guilty Plea' *The Annals of the American Academy of Political and Social Science* Vol. 374 (1967) pp. 70–81.

Royal Commission on the Police Cmd. 3297 (1929).

Royal Commission on the Police Cmnd. 1728 (1962).

A. Samuels 'Guilty Plea and Sentencing: Proposed Improvements' *Solicitors Journal* Vol. 115 (1971) pp. 120–2.

R. D. Seifman 'The Rise and Fall of Cain' *Criminal Law Review* (1976) pp. 556–60.

J. H. Skolnick 'Social Control in the Adversary System' *Journal of Conflict Resolution* Vol. 11 (1967) pp. 52–70.

J. C. Smith 'Questioning by the Police: Some Further Points—1' *Criminal Law Review* (1960) pp. 347–52.

J. M. Smith and W. P. Dale 'Legitimation of Plea Bargaining: Remedies for Broken Promises' *American Criminal Law Review* Vol. 11 (1973) pp. 771–99.

D. D. Sudnow 'Normal Crimes: Sociological Features of the Penal Code in a Public Defender's Office' *Social Problems* Vol. 12 (1965) pp. 255–76.

E. H. Sutherland and D. R. Cressey *Principles of Criminology* 6th edn, Lippincott (1960).

E. S. Thomas 'Plea Bargaining—the Clash Between Theory and Practice' *Loyola Law Review* Vol. 20 (1974) pp. 303–12.

D. A. Thomas 'Appellate Review of Sentences and the Development of Sentencing Policy: The English Experience' *Alabama Law Review* Vol. 20 (1968) pp. 193–201.

D. A. Thomas *Principles of Sentencing* Heinemann (1970).

P. Thomas 'An Exploration of Plea Bargaining' *Criminal Law Review* (1969) pp. 69–79.

P. Thomas 'Plea Bargaining and the Turner Case' *Criminal Law Review* (1970) pp. 559–66.

D. Thompson 'Questioning: A Comment' *Criminal Law Review* (1967) pp. 94–100.

125

University of Chicago Law Review, Note 'Official Inducements to Plead Guilty: Suggested Morals for a Marketplace' *University of Chicago Law Review* Vol. 32 (1964) pp. 167–87.

University of Richmond Law Review, Note 'Plea Bargaining: The Case for Reform' *Richmond University Law Review* Vol. 6 (1972) pp. 325–46.

D. R. Vetri 'Guilty Plea Bargaining: Compromises by Prosecutors to Secure Guilty Pleas' *University of Pennsylvania Law Review* Vol. 112 (1964) pp. 865–908.

R. G. Weintraub and R. Tough 'Lesser Pleas Considered' *Journal of Criminal Law, Criminology, and Police Science* Vol. 32 (1942) pp. 506–30.

D. J. West *The Habitual Prisoner* Macmillan (1963).

J. R. Wheatley 'Plea Bargaining—a Case for its Continuance' *Massachusetts Law Quarterly* Vol. 59 (1974) pp. 31–41.

W. S. White 'A Proposal for Reform of the Plea Bargaining Process' *University of Pennsylvania Law Review* Vol. 119 (1971) pp. 439–65.

P. A. Whitman 'Judicial Plea Bargaining' *Stanford Law Review* Vol. 19 (1967) pp. 1082–92.

Glanville Williams 'Questioning by the Police: Some Practical Considerations' *Criminal Law Review* (1960) pp. 325–46.

J. Wishingrad 'Plea Bargain in Historical Perspective' *Buffalo Law Review* Vol. 23 (1974) pp. 449–527.

Yale Law Journal 'The Influence of the Defendant's Plea on Judicial Determination of Sentence' *Yale Law Journal* Vol. 66 (1956) pp. 204–22.

Yale Law Journal 'Restructuring the Plea Bargain' *Yale Law Journal* Vol. 82 (1972) pp. 286–312.

M. Zander 'Access to a Solicitor in the Police Station' *Criminal Law Review* (1972a) pp. 342–50.

M. Zander 'Legal Advice and Criminal Appeals: A Survey of Prisoners, Prisons and Lawyers' *Criminal Law Review* (1972b) pp. 132–73.

M. Zander 'Are Too Many Professional Criminals Avoiding Conviction? —A Study in Britain's Two Busiest Courts' *Modern Law Review* Vol. 37 (1974) pp. 28–61.

INDEX OF AUTHORS

A